Creative Cooking
THE COSTCO WAY™

Two-Berry Tart with Chocolate Drizzle can be found on page 165.

Creative Cooking
THE COSTCO WAY™

Favorite recipes using Costco products

Tim Talevich
Editorial Director

With a foreword by
Lauren Purcell &
Anne Purcell Grissinger

Issaquah, Washington

Publisher:	David W. Fuller
Editorial Director:	Tim Talevich
Art Director:	Doris Winters
Associate Editor:	Judy Gouldthorpe
Graphic Designers:	Dawna Tessier Pat Armstrong
Photographers:	Darren Emmens Chris McArthur Tom Clements Devin Seferos
Food Stylists:	Amy Muzyka-McGuire Jane Morimoto Chris Jackson Joanne Naganawa
Kitchen Manager:	Linda Carey
Studio Assistant:	Rozarri Lynch
Business Manager:	Jane Klein-Shucklin
Advertising Manager:	Steve Trump
Advertising Assistant:	Leslie Hostak
Production Manager:	Pam Sather
Assistant Production Manager:	Antolin Matsuda
Color Specialist:	MaryAnne Robbers
Proofreader:	Shana McNally
Distribution:	Rossie Cruz

All photographs by Iridio Photography,
with the following exceptions:
Diamond Fruit Growers, 18 (top right)
Andrea Hillebrand, 103 (chef photo)
George Whiteside, 105 (chef photo)
Starbucks, 188

FIRST EDITION

Photography by Iridio Photography, Seattle
Printed by Choice Printing (Shanghai), Inc., China

ISBN 0-9722164-5-6
Library of Congress Control Number: 2005931691

45

58

94

154

$\mathcal{C}$ontents

Letter from Ginnie Roeglin   6

Foreword by Lauren Purcell &
Anne Purcell Grissinger   7

About This Book   8

❚ Breakfast   10

❚ Appetizers   24

❚ Salads and Soups   36

❚ Side Dishes   58

❚ Chef's Choice   68
Recipes created by some of America's
outstanding chefs using Costco products

❚ Entrées   106

❚ Desserts   154

❚ Beverages   182

Index   189

To Our Valued Members

At Costco, we're always seeking ways to add value to your membership. That's the spirit behind our products and our services. And that's the spirit behind this new book, *Creative Cooking The Costco Way*. We're delighted to offer you a copy as a way of saying thanks for your loyal membership.

As you might expect from Costco, *Creative Cooking The Costco Way* has a heavy emphasis on quality and value—whether it is what you buy or what you serve. Just as in our warehouses, the focus here is on the essentials, starting with breakfast and ending with dessert, all presented in fresh ways.

And, just as in our warehouses, there is always an unexpected treasure to be discovered, such as our special "Chef's Choice" section on page 68. We've also included recipes for appetizers, beverages, soups and salads and more, with the common themes being easy preparation and a great result.

You'll see from the recipes how easy it is to add creative touches to Costco products to make them "home-made." Your family and friends will be very impressed with your efforts!

This book has been made possible through the support of Costco's many suppliers. These are the same vendors who work so closely with our Costco buyers to constantly improve the quality and value of the food products we sell. At our request, they have come up with some great ways to prepare their specialties, all with an emphasis on creativity, simplicity and ease in the kitchen.

Costco has a long tradition as an innovator in food retailing, and we hope you will enjoy these recipes using some of our favorite products.

Bon appétit!

Ginnie Roeglin,
Senior Vice President,
E-commerce and Publishing

We have a confession to make: We can't seem to make it out of Costco having stuck to our shopping list. There we are in the checkout lane and poking out of our cart (or carts!) are a couple of racks of lamb that looked so tempting we had to grab them, or a big bag of limes we didn't intend to buy but which suddenly has us thinking: margaritas tonight! And are those fresh salmon fillets? Did they leap in there by themselves?

Strolling Costco's food aisles always inspires us to cook—and since we're buying in volume, our thoughts often turn to entertaining a crowd. A cocktail party starts to take shape in our heads, or we make a mental note to invite a few people over for dinner Saturday. Soon all that remains between us and an evening of good food and good friends is to figure out what to do with all those treasures!

That's where *Creative Cooking The Costco Way* comes in. If you're long on inspiration but not quite sure about execution, you'll find inventive ways to cook your favorite foods. Or flip through it before your next shopping trip and let it motivate you to try out a new-to-you dish. There's even a special section of recipes created by some of the country's best-known chefs, who were inspired, as we were, by the range and quality of food available at Costco. (We've offered up a few of our own recipes, too—you'll find out what we came up with for our racks of lamb on page 87.)

The ingenious ideas and glorious photographs in *Creative Cooking The Costco Way* can't help but make your mouth water and your chopping arm tingle in anticipation of the fantastic meals you can make. And if you're thinking about cooking for a crowd … we'd love to be invited!

Sisters Lauren Purcell, at right in the photo, and Anne Purcell Grissinger are the authors of Cocktail Parties, Straight Up! Easy Hors d'Oeuvres, Delicious Drinks, and Inspired Ideas for Entertaining with Style. *For more recipes and fun entertainment tips from this New York–based team, see their Web site,* www.purcellsisters.com.

Lauren Purcell

Anne P. Grissinger

About This Book ▌

This is the fourth volume in our *The Costco Way* cookbook series. As with last year's book, *Easy Cooking The Costco Way*, it is being distributed free to our members on a first-come, first-served basis the weekend after Thanksgiving as a token of our appreciation for their membership.

For *Creative Cooking The Costco Way* we have asked a number of America's outstanding chefs to team with some of our vendors to show off their delectable products to the best advantage. You will find these special dishes in the "Chef's Choice" section beginning on page 68. Each of these chefs has achieved national renown with cookbooks of their own, shows or appearances on The Food Network or exceptional restaurants. I want to thank them all for joining us in this exciting addition to our *The Costco Way* cookbooks.

The rest of the book is arranged according to type of dish, with sections for breakfast, appetizers, salads and soups, side dishes, entrées, desserts and beverages, the same approach we adopted with last year's book. To make finding what you are looking for as simple as possible, the index at the back of the book contains listings by vendor, recipe title and food item.

If you have friends and family who have not been able to obtain a copy of this book or *Easy Cooking The Costco Way*, you can direct them to the online versions at *www.costcoconnection.com*, where both books can be searched by keywords.

Every recipe in *Creative Cooking The Costco Way* has been identified with the vendor's name and logo. We want to thank each of them for their support of this book. Please note, however, that some branded products may not be sold in your part of the country. In such cases, you should substitute a similar product.

I hope you enjoy this token of our appreciation for your membership and that you will find it useful in your own creative cooking *The Costco Way*.

David W. Fuller,
Publisher

Note on Brands
Many of the recipes in this book were submitted by companies that hold copyrights to the recipes and/or trademark applications/registrations on the brands listed in the recipes. Each of the companies represented in this book asserts its ownership of the trademarks, applications/registrations and copyrights it holds on its company name, brands or recipes. Trademark, application/registration and copyright symbols have been eliminated from the titles and text of the recipes by the publishers for design and readability purposes only.

Creative Cooking
THE COSTCO WAY™

Breakfast

Strawberry and Ricotta Cheese Omelet
MICHAEL FOODS ◀

1/3 cup thinly sliced strawberries, plus more for garnish
1 teaspoon sugar
1/2 cup Kirkland Signature™ Egg Starts
Salt and pepper
1 tablespoon unsalted butter
2 tablespoons ricotta cheese
Cinnamon sugar

1. Combine 1/3 cup strawberries and sugar in a small bowl and set aside.
2. Pour eggs into a medium bowl and add salt and pepper to taste.
3. Heat a medium nonstick skillet with low, sloping sides over medium heat for 2 minutes. Add butter and swirl to coat pan. When butter stops sizzling, pour egg mixture into the center of the pan, reduce heat to low and cook until the bottom is set, about 10 seconds. Using a heatproof rubber spatula or wooden spoon, pull the set eggs at the edges of the pan toward the center, allowing the unset eggs to run from the center to the sides. Adjust heat if necessary so the bottom does not brown. Continue cooking until the eggs are soft-set—just a thin layer of unset moist egg should be visible on top—adjusting the heat so the bottom doesn't brown.
4. Slide pan off the heat. Spoon strawberries and ricotta onto the third of the omelet closest to the skillet handle. Using the spatula, fold the third of the omelet nearest the handle over the center third. Hold pan by the handle and tilt so the omelet rolls out of the pan and onto a plate seam side down.
5. Sprinkle generously with cinnamon sugar and serve. Garnish with additional sliced strawberries, if desired. Makes 1 serving.

Croissant Melt
EGGLAND'S BEST ▲

4 medium-sized croissants
2 plum tomatoes, thinly sliced
4 Eggland's Best* eggs
1 tablespoon milk
Salt
Freshly ground pepper
1 1/2 teaspoons butter
4 slices Havarti cheese, cut in half diagonally

1. Preheat oven to 350°F.
2. Cut croissants in half lengthwise and place the bottom halves on a baking sheet. Place tomato slices on croissant bottoms.
3. In a medium bowl, combine eggs, milk, and salt and pepper to taste; beat well.
4. In a medium skillet, melt butter over medium heat. Add the egg mixture and scramble until firm but not browned.
5. Spoon the scrambled eggs onto the croissant bottoms. Place a piece of cheese on the eggs and replace the top of each croissant. Top each croissant with another piece of cheese.
6. Bake for 3-4 minutes, or until heated through and the cheese is melted. Makes 4 servings.

Brands may vary by region; substitute a similar product.

Bacon and Cheddar Omelet Roll
NORCO RANCH/NuCAL FOODS/
WILCOX FARMS ◀

Parchment paper
1/2 cup Wilcox* cottage cheese
3/4 cup Wilcox* half-and-half
2 tablespoons all-purpose flour
1/4 teaspoon salt
12 Norco Ranch* or NuCal Foods* eggs
2 tablespoons Dijon mustard
6 ounces Cheddar cheese, grated (1 1/2 cups)
8 ounces bacon, cooked and crumbled (1 1/2 cups)

1. Preheat oven to 375°F.
2. Cut an 18-inch-long piece of parchment paper. Press into the bottom and up the sides of a 10-by-15 1/2-by-1 1/2-inch pan. Pinch the corners to prevent the egg mixture from running under the parchment paper.
3. Place cottage cheese and half-and-half in a blender and process for 20 seconds, or until well combined. Add flour and salt and blend for 20 seconds.
4. Add eggs to the blender and process until well incorporated and the mixture is lemon colored.
5. Pour the egg mixture into the prepared pan. Bake for 30-33 minutes, or until the omelet is puffy and golden.
6. Remove omelet from the oven; immediately spread with Dijon mustard. Sprinkle with 3/4 of the cheese; top with bacon. Starting on one short side, roll up jelly-roll fashion, removing parchment paper as you roll.
7. Garnish with the remaining cheese. Let stand for 5 minutes, until the cheese melts. Slice into wedges. Makes 8 servings.

Brands may vary by region; substitute a similar product.

Denver Omelet Bagel Panini
EINSTEIN BROS. BAGELS ▲

2 teaspoons butter, divided
1 tablespoon diced green bell pepper
1 tablespoon diced yellow onion
Cooking spray
1/2 cup beaten eggs or egg substitute
Salt and pepper
1 tablespoon shredded pizza cheese
1 Kirkland Signature plain bagel
1 slice Cheddar cheese
2 ounces sliced ham

1. Heat 1 teaspoon butter in a small pan over medium heat. Add bell pepper and onion; sauté until tender.
2. Lightly spray a 4-inch-diameter microwavable dish with cooking spray. Place sautéed pepper and onion in the dish. Add eggs, salt and pepper to taste and shredded pizza cheese. Microwave on high for approximately 1-1 1/2 minutes, or until eggs are cooked.
3. Cut bagel in half, brush with remaining butter, and grill in a sandwich grill or toast in a toaster.
4. Place Cheddar and ham on one side of bagel, add omelet and top with other bagel half. Makes 1 serving.

Breakfast

Breakfast Tostada with Eggo Waffles
KELLOGG'S

12 Eggo Waffles
12 eggs
3 cups sausage, cooked and crumbled
6 ounces tomatoes, diced
6 ounces Cheddar cheese, shredded
6 ounces Monterey Jack cheese, shredded
Salsa
Pepper of choice, for garnish (optional)

1. Preheat oven to 350°F.
2. Toast waffles.
3. Scramble eggs, folding in prepared sausage while cooking eggs.
4. Top toasted waffles with scrambled eggs and sausage, diced tomatoes, shredded Cheddar cheese and shredded Monterey Jack cheese.
5. Bake in the oven until the cheese is melted.
6. Serve with a side dish of salsa and garnish with slices of jalapeño or other pepper. Makes 12 servings.

Breakfast Casserole
JIMMY DEAN ▼

1 pound Jimmy Dean* Pork Sausage
10 eggs, lightly beaten
3 cups milk
2 teaspoons dry mustard
1 teaspoon salt
6 cups cubed bread
1/2 teaspoon ground black pepper
2 cups sharp Cheddar cheese, shredded
1/2 cup sliced mushrooms (optional)
1 medium tomato, seeded and chopped (optional)
1/2 cup thinly sliced green onions (optional)

1. Preheat oven to 325°F.
2. In a large skillet, cook sausage over medium-high heat, stirring frequently, until thoroughly cooked and no longer pink.
3. In a large mixing bowl, combine eggs, milk, mustard and salt; stir well.
4. Distribute half the bread cubes evenly in a buttered 9-by-13-by-2-inch baking dish. Sprinkle with half the pepper, half the cheese, half the sausage and half of each optional ingredient. Repeat layering, using remaining bread cubes, pepper, cheese, sausage and optional ingredients. Pour egg mixture evenly over casserole.
5. Bake, uncovered, for 55-60 minutes, or until eggs are set. Tent with foil if the top begins to brown too quickly. Makes 6 servings.

Tip: This can be assembled and refrigerated for up to 12 hours before baking.

Brands may vary by region; substitute a similar product.

Nectarine French Toast Soufflé
WESPAK

8 cups 1/2-inch bread cubes, crusts removed

1/2 cup butter, softened

8 ounces cream cheese, softened

1/2 cup maple syrup, plus more for serving

12 eggs

3 cups half-and-half

1 1/2 teaspoons vanilla extract

Ground cinnamon

6-8 WesPak* nectarines, peeled and sliced

1 tablespoon lemon juice

2 tablespoons sugar

Confectioners' sugar

1. Preheat oven to 350°F.

2. Butter a 9-by-13-inch baking dish. Fill two-thirds full with bread cubes.

3. In a bowl, combine butter, cream cheese and 1/2 cup maple syrup; beat until smooth. Spoon evenly over bread cubes.

4. Combine eggs, half-and-half and vanilla; beat until well blended. Pour over bread cubes. Dust with cinnamon. Can be stored overnight in the refrigerator.

5. Bake for 45-55 minutes, or until the center is firm.

6. Meanwhile, combine nectarines, lemon juice and sugar in a bowl.

7. Top the soufflé with sliced nectarines and dust with confectioners' sugar. Serve with warm maple syrup. Makes 10 servings.

* Brands may vary by region; substitute a similar product.

Healthy French Toast
MILTON'S

2 eggs (or equivalent of egg substitute)

1/2 cup vanilla soy milk

1 teaspoon ground cinnamon

1/2 teaspoon grated nutmeg

Cooking spray

5 slices Milton's Healthy Multi-Grain Bread, cut in half

Maple syrup or all-fruit jam

1. In a bowl, beat together eggs, soy milk, cinnamon and nutmeg.

2. Coat a frying pan or griddle with cooking spray; heat over medium-high heat.

3. Soak bread in the egg mixture for a few seconds. Cook for a few minutes on each side, or until golden brown.

4. Serve with maple syrup or all-fruit jam. Makes 2-3 servings.

Oatmeal Raisin Cookie Pancakes with Maple Syrup Frosting
J&J SNACK FOODS ▼

MAPLE SYRUP FROSTING
3/4 cup butter, softened
3 cups sifted powdered sugar
1/2 cup maple syrup
1/4 cup milk

1 cup dry pancake mix
1 cup milk
2 large eggs
2 tablespoons vegetable oil
1/2 cup raisins
16 Kirkland Signature Oatmeal Raisin Cookies

1. Prepare Maple Syrup Frosting: In a large mixing bowl, combine butter, powdered sugar, maple syrup and milk. Mix until well blended and set aside to thicken.

2. In a large mixing bowl, combine dry pancake mix, milk, eggs, 1 tablespoon vegetable oil and 1/4 cup raisins.

3. Crumble cookies and add to pancake batter, stirring until cookies are completely covered and batter is lumpy. Let stand for 2 minutes.

4. Add 1 tablespoon oil to griddle and heat over medium heat. Pour 1/4 cup of batter onto griddle for each pancake, flatten and cook until golden brown.

5. Top pancakes with Maple Syrup Frosting and raisins. If desired, sprinkle with powdered sugar. Serve immediately. Makes 8-10 servings (16-20 pancakes).

Grilled Croissants with Orange Caramel Sauce
VIE DE FRANCE ▲

7 large eggs

1 ¹/₂ cups whole milk

2 teaspoons vanilla extract

¹/₂ teaspoon ground cinnamon

¹/₄ teaspoon grated nutmeg

2 tablespoons unsalted butter

8 Vie de France butter croissants, sliced in half lengthwise

Maple syrup

ORANGE CARAMEL SAUCE

1 ¹/₂ cups sugar

³/₄ cup orange juice

1. Preheat oven to 200°F.

2. In a large bowl, whisk together eggs, milk, vanilla, cinnamon and nutmeg. Set aside.

3. Melt butter in a skillet over medium-high heat. Dip each croissant half in batter until thoroughly soaked. Cook in the skillet until golden brown, 2-3 minutes on each side. Place on a baking sheet in the oven to keep warm.

4. Prepare Orange Caramel Sauce: Cook sugar in a saucepan over medium heat until it begins to melt. Continue to cook, stirring occasionally with a fork, until melted into a deep caramel.

5. Remove from heat and *carefully* pour the orange juice into the caramel. Return pan to burner and cook over medium heat, stirring, until caramel is dissolved. Let cool to warm.

6. Drizzle croissants with warm sauce and maple syrup. Makes 8 servings.

Breakfast Pear and Bacon Cheese Sandwich
DIAMOND FRUIT GROWERS ▲

4 slices sourdough, whole wheat or white bread

4 slices Cheddar cheese

1 firm but ripe Diamond Fruit Growers* Bartlett, Anjou or Bosc pear, quartered lengthwise, cored and sliced (peel pears if desired)

4 slices cooked bacon

2 tablespoons butter, softened

1. Place 2 slices of bread on a work surface and top each slice with a piece of cheese. Arrange pear slices on top of each piece of cheese.

2. Add 2 slices of bacon and then top with another piece of cheese. Place a slice of bread on top and butter the top slices of bread with half of the butter.

3. Preheat a griddle or large skillet. Place the sandwiches buttered side down on the hot griddle or pan. Butter the top side of the sandwiches. Grill until nicely browned on one side and then flip and brown the other side.

4. Cut each sandwich in half and serve immediately. Makes 2 sandwiches.

Brands may vary by region; substitute a similar product.

Diamond
FRUIT GROWERS, INC.

Orange and Apple Breakfast Knots
SUNNY COVE ▼

4 medium Granny Smith apples
2 11-ounce packages refrigerated breadsticks
2 Sunny Cove navel oranges
1/3 cup sugar
1/2 teaspoon ground cinnamon

1. Preheat oven to 375°F.

2. Peel and core apples, cut in half and then cut each half into 1/4-inch-thick slices.

3. Unroll breadstick dough; cut the strips in half. Place 3-4 apple slices in the middle of each strip of dough; wrap and tie in a knot. Arrange knots in a 9-by-13-inch pan.

4. Grate 1 teaspoon of orange peel; set aside. Juice the oranges; pour 2/3 cup juice into the bottom of the pan but not over the knots.

5. In a small bowl, combine grated peel, sugar and cinnamon; spoon over the knots.

6. Bake for 25-30 minutes, or until golden brown. Serve warm with a drizzle of syrup from the pan. Makes 12 servings (24 knots).

Fruit Bowl with Raspberry Vinaigrette
KIRSCHENMAN/MAS MELONS & GRAPES ▼

10 ounces frozen raspberries, thawed

1/3 cup sugar

1 tablespoon red wine vinegar

2 tablespoons lemon juice

1/8 teaspoon salt

1 dash grated nutmeg

1/2 cup olive oil

1 Mas Melons & Grapes* cantaloupe

1 Mas Melons & Grapes* honeydew melon

1/2 Mas Melons & Grapes* seedless watermelon

2 cups Kirschenman* red or green grapes

1. In a blender, puree raspberries and sugar.
2. Blend in vinegar and lemon juice.
3. Add salt and nutmeg; blend for 10 seconds.
4. Gradually add olive oil while continuing to blend.
5. Cut up melons and grapes and place in a large bowl. Pour dressing over the fruit and stir to combine. Makes 8-10 servings.

Brands may vary by region; substitute a similar product.

Coffee Banana Bread
KIRKLAND SIGNATURE/SARA LEE

3 cups flour
2 teaspoons baking soda
2 teaspoons baking powder
1/4 teaspoon salt
2 cups sugar
1/4 cup margarine, softened
2 eggs
1 1/2 teaspoons vanilla extract
1 3/4 cups hot brewed Kirkland Signature coffee
1 1/2 cups mashed ripe bananas

1. Preheat oven to 350°F.

2. Mix flour, baking soda, baking powder and salt in a medium bowl.

3. In a separate large bowl, mix sugar, margarine, eggs and vanilla. Add dry ingredients to wet ingredients. Slowly add hot coffee, mixing until combined. Add mashed bananas and blend thoroughly.

4. Pour into 2 greased and floured 5-by-9-inch loaf pans. Bake for 1 hour, or until a toothpick inserted in the center comes out clean. Makes 2 loaves.

SaraLee Coffee & Tea
NORTH AMERICA

Bing Cherry Cream Cheese Nut Bread
M&R

3/4 cup butter, softened
1 8-ounce package cream cheese, softened
1 cup sugar
2 eggs
3 cups flour
1 teaspoon baking powder
1 teaspoon baking soda
1/2 teaspoon salt
1 8-ounce can crushed pineapple
2 cups pitted M&R* Bing cherries, coarsely chopped
1 teaspoon vanilla extract
1 cup coarsely chopped pecans, toasted
Confectioners' sugar, for garnish

1. Preheat oven to 350°F. Grease and flour two 5-by-9-inch loaf pans.

2. In a large bowl, cream butter and cream cheese. Add sugar and eggs and mix well.

3. Sift together flour, baking powder, baking soda and salt.

4. Gradually add flour mixture, pineapple and cherries to butter mixture. Add vanilla and mix well. Stir in pecans.

5. Pour into prepared pans. Bake for 50 minutes, or until a toothpick inserted in the center comes out clean.

6. Cool in pans on a wire rack for 10 minutes. Remove to the wire rack to cool completely. Sprinkle with confectioners' sugar before slicing, if desired. Makes 2 loaves.

Brands may vary by region; substitute a similar product.

Blueberry Pecan Cluster Muffins
NEWMAN'S OWN/KERRY

1 cup boiling water
2 1/2 teaspoons baking soda
3 cups Kirkland Signature/Newman's Own Wild Blueberry
   Pecan Cluster Cereal
2 cups buttermilk
1/2 cup shortening
1 cup sugar
2 eggs
2 1/2 cups flour
1/2 teaspoon salt

1. Preheat oven to 375°F.
2. Mix boiling water and baking soda; let cool.
3. Pour cereal into a large bowl. Add buttermilk and let stand
for 10 minutes.
4. Cream shortening and sugar. Beat in eggs one at a time.
5. Sift together flour and salt. Add to creamed mixture alternately
with cooled water/soda mixture. Stir in cereal mixture.
6. Grease muffin pans. Scoop batter into muffin cups. Bake for
20-30 minutes, or until golden brown. Makes 24 muffins.
Tip: Muffin mix will keep in the refrigerator for 1 week
in a covered container.

Blueberry Pecan Cluster
Breakfast Parfait
NEWMAN'S OWN/KERRY

2 8-ounce cups of your favorite yogurt
1 1/2 cups Kirkland Signature/Newman's Own Wild Blueberry
   Pecan Cluster Cereal
1 ripe banana, sliced
2 teaspoons honey (optional)
1/2 teaspoon ground cinnamon (optional)

1. Use 2 wine goblets or clear glass bowls.
2. Place a layer of yogurt in each goblet, then a layer of cereal and a layer
of banana. Continue layering, ending with cereal on top.
3. Top with a drizzle of honey and a sprinkle of cinnamon for a delicious
start to your day. Makes 2 servings.
Tip: Kids love this great-looking combination. Remember, breakfast
is the most important meal of the day.

Harvest Fruit Bars
QUAKER/TROPICANA ▼

1 6-ounce package diced dried mixed fruit bits
1 cup chopped banana (about 2 medium)
²/₃ cup Tropicana Orange Juice*
1 ¹/₂ teaspoons apple pie spice or ground cinnamon, divided
1 ³/₄ cups whole wheat flour or all-purpose flour
1 ¹/₂ cups Quaker Oats (quick or old-fashioned, uncooked)
¹/₂ pound (2 sticks) margarine or butter, softened
1 cup firmly packed brown sugar
¹/₂ cup chopped nuts

1. Preheat oven to 375°F.

2. In a medium bowl, combine dried fruit, banana, orange juice and 1 teaspoon apple pie spice; set aside.

3. In a medium bowl, combine flour, oats and remaining ¹/₂ teaspoon apple pie spice; mix well.

4. In a large bowl, beat margarine and sugar together with an electric mixer until creamy. Add oat mixture and beat until crumbly.

5. Reserve ³/₄ cup mixture for topping. Press remaining oat mixture onto bottom of a 9-by-13-inch baking pan. Bake for 13-15 minutes, or until light golden brown.

6. Spread fruit evenly over crust to within ¹/₄ inch of edge. Add nuts to reserved oat mixture and mix well. Sprinkle evenly over fruit and pat down lightly.

7. Bake for 16-20 minutes, or until golden brown. Cool completely; cut into bars. Store loosely covered. Makes 32 bars.

*If using old-fashioned oats, decrease orange juice to ¹/₂ cup.

Appetizers

Italian Stuffed Mushrooms
CARDILE BROTHERS ◄

18 large Cardile Brothers* mushrooms
1 tablespoon olive oil
¹/₄ cup minced onion
1 garlic clove, minced
¹/₄ cup finely chopped walnuts
1 shredded wheat biscuit, crushed
1 tablespoon grated Parmesan cheese
¹/₂ teaspoon dried Italian herb seasoning
Freshly ground black pepper
¹/₂ teaspoon paprika (optional)

1. Preheat oven to 350°F.
2. Clean mushrooms with a vegetable brush or wipe with a damp cloth. Remove and finely chop stems.
3. Heat oil in a nonstick skillet over medium-high heat. Sauté chopped mushroom stems, onion, garlic and walnuts until onion is tender, 4-5 minutes. Remove from heat. Stir in shredded wheat, Parmesan, herb seasoning and pepper to taste.
4. Stuff mushroom caps, packing the mixture firmly. Arrange mushrooms in a shallow baking dish. Sprinkle tops with paprika. Bake for 20-25 minutes, or until mushrooms are tender. Makes 6 servings.

Brands may vary by region; substitute a similar product.

Cardile Bros.

Bacon-Wrapped Shrimp
MAPLE LEAF ▲

8 large shrimp, shelled and deveined
3-4 slices Maple Leaf bacon, cut into 2- to 3-inch sections

SPICY ORANGE SAUCE
3 tablespoons orange marmalade
1 hot red chile, stemmed and chopped
2 green onions, white and green parts, chopped
2 tablespoons chopped fresh cilantro
2 tablespoons extra-virgin olive oil
Salt and pepper

1. Preheat the broiler.
2. To prepare Spicy Orange Sauce, in a bowl stir together marmalade, chile, green onions, cilantro, olive oil, and salt and pepper to taste.
3. Wrap each shrimp in a section of bacon and secure with a toothpick.
4. Place shrimp on a baking sheet and broil, turning once, until bacon is crisp and shrimp are cooked through, 2-3 minutes each side.
5. Arrange on a platter and serve immediately with Spicy Orange Sauce or your favorite dipping sauce. Makes 8 servings.

Dungeness Dan's
Crab Cakes Italienne
PACIFIC SEAFOOD ▲

1 pound Dungeness crab meat (2-3 crabs)
1 teaspoon minced garlic
1/2 cup grated Parmesan cheese
1/2 cup Italian-style dry bread crumbs
2 teaspoons chopped fresh parsley
1/4 teaspoon ground pepper
1 egg, lightly beaten
2 tablespoons plus 1/2 cup mayonnaise
1 teaspoon lemon juice
1/4 cup ketchup
4 tablespoons olive oil

1. Combine crab, garlic, Parmesan, bread crumbs, parsley and pepper. Gently blend in egg, 2 tablespoons mayonnaise and lemon juice. Form into 16 patties about 3/4 inch thick.
2. For an easy sauce, combine 1/2 cup mayonnaise and ketchup.
3. Heat olive oil in a large skillet on medium-high heat. When oil is hot, add patties and cook on each side until golden brown. Serve immediately with sauce. Makes 16 appetizers.

Spicy Crab Melt
GRACE BAKING ▲

6 ounces cream cheese, softened
2 cups crabmeat
1/2 cup sliced green onions
2 cups shredded Parmesan cheese, divided
1 tablespoon lemon juice
1 tablespoon white wine
1 tablespoon horseradish
2 teaspoons hot pepper sauce
1 loaf Grace Baking* Pugliese artisan bread
Olive oil
Salt and pepper

1. In a bowl, mix cream cheese, crabmeat, green onions, 1 cup Parmesan, lemon juice, white wine, horseradish and hot pepper sauce.
2. Cut bread into 18 slices. Brush each slice lightly with olive oil and sprinkle with salt and pepper to taste. Toast slices under a broiler until lightly golden.
3. Spread 1 1/2-2 tablespoons of topping on each warm slice. Sprinkle with remaining shredded Parmesan. If desired, place under broiler for a couple of minutes to melt the cheese. Makes 8-10 servings.

* Brands may vary by region; substitute a similar product.

Chili Lime Shrimp
CONAGRA

2 tablespoons Hunt's Tomato Paste
2 tablespoons Asian chili garlic paste
Pam Original No-Stick Cooking Spray
1 pound medium shrimp (16/20 count), peeled and deveined
1 lime, cut into wedges

1. Combine tomato paste and chili paste in a small bowl.

2. Spray a wok or large skillet with cooking spray; heat over high heat for 1 minute. Add shrimp and cook for 5 minutes, or until shrimp turn pink, stirring frequently.

3. Add tomato paste mixture to shrimp and toss to coat evenly.

4. Divide shrimp evenly among 4 plates. Squeeze 1 lime wedge over each serving. Garnish with additional lime wedges. Makes 4 servings.

ConAgra Foods®

Sushi Dipping Sauces
OKAMI ▲

Use these dipping sauces with Okami* Sushi, available in your local Costco deli:

CREAMY CHILI/SESAME SAUCE

$1/2$ cup mayonnaise
$1/4$ cup sugar
$1/4$ cup white vinegar
2 tablespoons soy sauce
2 teaspoons chili sauce
1 teaspoon Asian sesame oil

Combine all ingredients and blend well. Makes 4 servings.

SOY DIPPING SAUCE

$1/4$ cup soy sauce
$1/4$ cup sugar
$1/4$ cup white vinegar
1 tablespoon corn oil
1 tablespoon chopped green onion

Combine all ingredients and blend well. Makes 4 servings.

* Brands may vary by region; substitute a similar product.

Okami™
The "Anytime" Meal

Sweet Mini Peppers Stuffed with Tuna and Salmon Tartare
WILSONBATIZ ▲

3 ounces fresh tuna, pureed
3 ounces fresh salmon, pureed
$1/3$ cup pitted black olives, finely chopped
$1/3$ cup chopped ginger in syrup
1 teaspoon soy sauce
1 teaspoon rice vinegar
1 teaspoon balsamic vinegar
1 teaspoon sugar
$1 1/2$ teaspoons Asian sesame oil
Salt
Pepper

4-6 Divine Flavor* Babylicious peppers, halved and seeded
Assorted lettuce leaves
Furikake (Japanese seasoning mix of sesame seeds and flavorings)

DRESSING
$1/2$ cup water
1 teaspoon sugar
2 pieces star anise, crushed
1 teaspoon saffron threads

1. In a bowl, combine tuna, salmon, olives, ginger, soy sauce, vinegars, sugar, sesame oil, and salt and pepper to taste.
2. To prepare the dressing, combine all ingredients in a small saucepan and cook over medium-low heat until slightly reduced.
3. Place half peppers on lettuce leaves and stuff with the tuna and salmon tartare. Pour dressing over peppers. Sprinkle with furikake. Makes 2-4 servings.

* Brands may vary by region; substitute a similar product.

WILSONBATIZ.

Caribbean Shrimp Dip
MARGARITAVILLE SHRIMP ▲

1 1.7-pound package Margaritaville Island Lime Shrimp*
2 tablespoons olive oil
1 1/2 cups thinly sliced green bell peppers
1 1/2 cups thinly sliced red bell peppers
2 8-ounce packages cream cheese, softened
1/2 cup heavy cream
1/2 cup chopped green onions
1/2 cup chopped fresh cilantro

1. Cook shrimp according to package directions. When slightly cooled, chop the shrimp into bite-size pieces.
2. In a separate pan, heat olive oil over medium heat and sauté bell peppers for 5 minutes, or until soft. Add cream cheese and cream, stirring briskly to blend. Once blended, stir in green onions, cilantro, shrimp and its sauce. Pour into a serving crock.
3. Serve with warm toasted pita triangles, grilled French bread slices, bagel chips, crackers or tortilla chips. Makes 8-10 servings.

Brands may vary by region; substitute a similar product.

Cucumber Dip
SCHREIBER ▲

1 pound Raskas* cream cheese, softened
1 cup sour cream
2 tablespoons milk
2 teaspoons grated onion
1/2 teaspoon Worcestershire sauce
2/3 cup finely chopped cucumber

1. Combine cream cheese, sour cream, milk, onion and Worcestershire sauce in a bowl, mixing until well blended.
2. Stir in cucumber.
3. Chill for several hours or overnight. Serve with vegetable dippers or chips. Makes 6-8 servings.

Brands may vary by region; substitute a similar product.

SCHREIBER ™

Red, White and Blueberry Cheese Spread
MARIANI ▲

2 8-ounce packages cream cheese, softened
2 tablespoons Cointreau or Triple Sec
1 tablespoon lemon juice
$^1/_2$ teaspoon Lawry's Seasoned Salt
1 tablespoon honey
1 cup crushed pineapple, drained
$^1/_3$ cup Mariani* dried blueberries (or dried cherries), plus more
    for garnish
1 cup finely chopped red bell pepper
Fresh herbs, for garnish

1. Beat cream cheese in a mixing bowl until smooth. Add Cointreau, lemon juice, seasoned salt, honey, pineapple and $^1/_3$ cup blueberries; mix well.
2. Place cheese mixture in the center of a piece of plastic wrap. Bring the corners up to meet and seal around the cheese, molding the mixture into a ball. Refrigerate overnight.
3. Remove from the refrigerator and form once again into a ball. The mixture will be stiff and easy to mold. Remove plastic and roll cheese ball in chopped red bell pepper to cover.
4. Garnish with fresh herbs and dried blueberries (or cherries). Serve with crackers. Makes 24 servings.

* Brands may vary by region; substitute a similar product.

Golden Artichoke Dip
LIPTON/HELLMANN'S ▲

1 envelope Lipton Recipe Secrets Golden Onion or Onion Soup Mix*
1 14-ounce can artichoke hearts, drained and chopped
1 cup Hellmann's or Best Foods Real Mayonnaise
1 8-ounce container sour cream
1 cup shredded Swiss or mozzarella cheese (about 4 ounces)

1. Preheat oven to 350°F.
2. In a 1-quart casserole, combine all ingredients.
3. Bake for 30 minutes, or until heated through.
4. Serve with your favorite dippers. Makes 3 cups.

Variation: For a cold Golden Artichoke Dip, omit Swiss cheese. Stir in, if desired, $^1/_4$ cup grated Parmesan cheese. Do not bake.

Tip: This recipe is also terrific with Lipton Recipe Secrets Savory Herb & Garlic or Onion Mushroom Soup Mix.

* Brands may vary by region; substitute a similar product.

Tomato Crostini
DARE FOODS ▼

$^1/_2$ cup chopped yellow cherry tomatoes
$^1/_2$ cup chopped red cherry tomatoes
$^1/_4$ cup fresh basil leaves, finely chopped
2 garlic cloves: 1 finely minced, 1 cut in half
Sea salt and pepper
2 tablespoons extra-virgin olive oil
$^1/_2$ tablespoon white balsamic vinegar
12-15 Breton* crackers
Basil leaves, for garnish

1. In a medium bowl, combine tomatoes, chopped basil, minced garlic, and salt and pepper to taste.

2. Place olive oil and vinegar in a small jar, cover and shake to combine thoroughly. Pour dressing over the tomato mixture and refrigerate, preferably for 30 minutes.

3. Rub garlic halves over the crackers, then spoon on the tomato mixture. Garnish each with a single basil leaf. Serve immediately. Makes 3-5 servings.

Variation: After rubbing crackers with garlic, place crackers on a cookie sheet covered with aluminum foil. Spoon tomato mixture onto crackers and top with thinly shaved Parmesan cheese. Broil just until the cheese melts, being careful not to burn the crackers. Serve warm.

* Brands may vary by region; substitute a similar product.

Taquitos with Bean Sauce
DELIMEX ▲

1 cup heavy whipping cream
1/2 cup refried beans
1/4 cup red chile enchilada sauce
4 thin slices ham
1/4 cup chicken broth
1/4 teaspoon ground cumin
18-20 Delimex* Chicken or Beef Corn Taquitos
Shredded Cheddar and Monterey Jack cheese

1. Preheat oven to 400°F.
2. Place cream, refried beans, enchilada sauce, ham, chicken broth and cumin in a blender or food processor and blend until creamy.
3. Place frozen taquitos in a 9-by-13-inch baking dish. Pour bean sauce over taquitos.
4. Cover baking dish with foil. Bake for 20 minutes, or until heated through.
5. Sprinkle with grated cheese and serve. Makes 4 servings.

Brands may vary by region; substitute a similar product.

Santa Fe Corn & Black Bean Salsa
DEL MONTE ▲

1 15-ounce can S&W* Black Beans, rinsed and drained
1 15 1/4-ounce can S&W* Whole Kernel Corn, drained
1 14 1/2-ounce can S&W* Diced Tomatoes, drained
1 teaspoon ground cumin
2 tablespoons fresh lime juice
1/4 cup chopped green onions
1/3 cup chopped fresh cilantro
1-2 tablespoons minced jalapeño pepper (to taste)

1. Combine all ingredients.
2. Serve with tortilla chips. Makes 12 servings.

Brands may vary by region; substitute a similar product.

Fiesta Platter with Spicy Mango Salsa
DON MIGUEL MEXICAN FOODS ▲

8 Don Miguel Rolled Chicken & Cheese Quesadillas*
25 Don Miguel Shredded Beef Mini Tacos*
8 Don Miguel Chipotle Chicken Flautas*

SPICY MANGO SALSA
2 mangoes, peeled and cut into small cubes
1 large red onion, diced
1 small bunch cilantro, chopped
1 red bell pepper, diced
1 serrano or jalapeño pepper, chopped (2 if you like it really spicy)
Juice of 1 lime
$1/2$ teaspoon minced garlic
Dash of salt
Freshly ground pepper (to taste)

1. Prepare Spicy Mango Salsa: Blend all ingredients in a serving bowl. Refrigerate for an hour.
2. Preheat oven to 400°F.
3. Place quesadillas, mini tacos and flautas on an ungreased cookie sheet and bake for 15 minutes. Makes 8 servings.
Tip: Try Spicy Mango Salsa with any of the other delicious Don Miguel appetizers such as our Shredded Steak or Chicken Mini Tacos, or Shredded Steak & Cheese Flautas.

* Brands may vary by region; substitute a similar product.

Quesadillas with Roasted Pepper & Jalapeño Hommus
HANNAH INTERNATIONAL ▲

Cooking oil or spray
1 pound boneless sirloin steak, sliced across the grain into $1/8$-inch strips
4 ounces white onion, thinly sliced
1 tablespoon pine nuts
1 container Hannah* Roasted Pepper & Jalapeño Hommus
8 flour tortillas
1 cup grated Monterey Jack cheese
Handful of fresh cilantro leaves, roughly chopped

1. Lightly oil a large nonstick frying pan and heat over medium-high heat. Add beef and onion and sauté until cooked to taste. Remove from the pan.
2. Add pine nuts to the pan and cook over medium heat for a few minutes, until they turn golden. Remove from the pan.
3. Spread a generous amount of hommus on 4 tortillas. Top with beef and onions, then grated cheese and pine nuts. Sprinkle with cilantro to taste. Place another tortilla directly on top.
4. Lightly coat a nonstick pan with oil and heat over medium heat. Cook each quesadilla for 1-2 minutes per side. Cut into wedges and serve warm. Makes 8 servings.

* Brands may vary by region; substitute a similar product.

Sausage-Cheese Balls
BISQUICK ▲

3 cups Original Bisquick mix

1 pound uncooked bulk pork sausage

4 cups shredded Cheddar cheese (16 ounces)

1/2 cup grated Parmesan cheese

1/2 cup milk

1/2 teaspoon dried rosemary leaves, crumbled

1 1/2 teaspoons chopped fresh parsley or 1/2 teaspoon
    dried parsley flakes

1. Heat oven to 350°F. Lightly grease a 15-by-10-by-1-inch pan.

2. Stir together all ingredients until well mixed, using your hands
if necessary. Shape mixture into 1-inch balls. Place in the pan.

3. Bake for 20-25 minutes, or until browned. Immediately remove from
the pan. Serve warm. Makes 34 servings (8 1/2 dozen).

High Altitude: (3,500-6,500 feet) Preheat oven to 375°F. Use 2 1/2 cups
Bisquick mix. Stir 1/2 cup all-purpose flour into Bisquick.

Betty's Tip: Get a jump start on your party. Make these tasty nibbles up
to a day ahead of time and refrigerate; bake as directed. Or cover and
freeze unbaked balls for up to 1 month. Bake frozen balls for 25-30 minutes,
or until browned.

Spinach Blue Cheese Flatbread
KIRKLAND SIGNATURE ▲

1 loaf Kirkland Signature Garlic Butter Flatbread or
    Roasted Garlic Bread*

5 tablespoons olive oil

8 shallots, minced

2 10-ounce packages frozen spinach, thawed and squeezed dry

1 teaspoon cayenne pepper

1 cup crumbled blue cheese

1/2 cup chopped roasted red bell pepper

1. Preheat oven to 375°F.

2. Bake bread on a baking sheet for 10 minutes.

3. Heat olive oil in a large sauté pan over medium heat. Add shallots
and cook for 5 minutes.

4. Stir in spinach and cayenne pepper.

5. Transfer mixture to a large bowl. Stir in blue cheese.

6. Spread spinach mixture onto bread. Sprinkle evenly with
chopped peppers.

7. Bake for 15-20 minutes, or until cheese is melted and bread begins
to brown. Remove from the oven and slice. Makes 10-12 servings.

Variation: Add 6 slices cooked and chopped bacon to the
spinach mixture.

* Brands may vary by region; substitute a similar product.

Bagel Bites with Dipping Sauce
ORE-IDA

30-40 Ore-Ida* Bagel Bites, deluxe or kosher
16 ounces cream cheese, softened
1 14-ounce jar pizza sauce
1 medium onion, chopped
1 2 1/4-ounce can sliced ripe olives (optional)
1 8-ounce package sliced pepperoni, chopped
8 ounces (2 cups) shredded mozzarella cheese

1. Prepare Bagel Bites according to package directions.

2. Spread cream cheese in the bottom of a slow cooker.

3. Combine pizza sauce, onion, olives and pepperoni; spread on
top of the cream cheese.

4. Sprinkle with pizza cheese and cook on low until the cheese melts. (May
also be baked in oven at 350° for 10-15 minutes or until cheese melts).

5. Serve Bagel Bites with the dip. Makes 8-10 servings.

* Brands may vary by region; substitute a similar product.

Grilled Pineapple, Ham and Marinated Ciliegine Skewers
MOZZARELLA FRESCA

1/2 fresh pineapple, peeled and cored
2 pounds Mozzarella Fresca* marinated fresh mozzarella balls
    (cherry-size)
3/4 pound ham, cut in bite-size chunks
16 bamboo skewers

1. Cut pineapple into bite-size chunks and grill until grill marks are present.

2. Thread pineapple, mozzarella and ham onto skewers, using approximately
5-6 mozzarella balls per skewer.

3. Drizzle with the marinade from the mozzarella. Cover and refrigerate
for up to 6 hours, or serve immediately.

4. To serve, stick skewers into a pineapple shell. Makes 16 servings.

Tip: Red, green and yellow bell peppers, cut into bite-size pieces, can also
be included on the skewers.

* Brands may vary by region; substitute a similar product.

Mozzarella Fresca
Family of Fresh Italian Cheeses

Salads and Soups

Cherry Salad Rubies and Greens
STEMILT GROWERS ◀

$^1/_3$ cup orange juice

2 tablespoons olive oil

2 tablespoons honey

$^1/_2$ teaspoon salt

Freshly ground black pepper to taste

1 5-ounce bag baby spinach or mixed salad greens

3 cups Stemilt* sweet cherries, pitted

2 cups sliced hothouse cucumber

$^1/_2$ cup finely diced red onion

1. Whisk together orange juice, olive oil, honey, salt and pepper.

2. Place spinach, cherries, cucumber and onion in a salad bowl.

3. Add dressing to salad and toss to coat. Makes 6 servings.

Brands may vary by region; substitute a similar product.

Fresh Cherry Picnic Salad
RAINIER FRUIT ▲

1 cup sugar snap peas

2 cups pitted Rainier Fruit* Northwest fresh sweet cherries

1 medium cucumber, halved, seeded and cut in $^1/_2$-inch slices

1 cup red radishes cut into wedge-shaped pieces

3 tablespoons white wine vinegar

2 tablespoons balsamic vinegar

$^1/_2$ teaspoon sesame oil

$^3/_4$ teaspoon salt

$^1/_2$ teaspoon toasted sesame seeds

$^1/_2$ teaspoon grated fresh ginger

$^1/_8$ teaspoon freshly ground black pepper

1. Blanch peas in boiling salted water for 1 minute. Plunge into iced water to cool, then drain.

2. Mix cherries, cucumber, radishes and peas in a salad bowl.

3. Combine vinegars, sesame oil, salt, sesame seeds, ginger and pepper in a small bowl and mix well. Pour over cherry mixture and toss to coat.

4. Marinate salad, refrigerated, for at least 1 hour. Makes 4-6 servings.

Brands may vary by region; substitute a similar product.

Cranberry Almond Spinach Salad
BOSKOVICH FARMS ▲

1 tablespoon butter
3/4 cup blanched, slivered almonds
1 pound Boskovich Farms* Fresh 'N' Quick Spinach
1 cup sweetened dried cranberries
4 ounces feta cheese, crumbled
2 tablespoons toasted sesame seeds
1 tablespoon poppy seeds
1/2 cup sugar
2 teaspoons minced onion
1/4 teaspoon paprika
1/4 cup white wine vinegar
1/4 cup cider vinegar
1/2 cup vegetable oil

1. Melt butter in a small pan over medium heat. Add almonds and cook until lightly toasted. Remove from heat and set aside to cool.

2. Chop or tear spinach into bite-size pieces and place in a large salad bowl.

3. Add toasted almonds, cranberries and feta.

4. To make dressing, whisk together sesame seeds, poppy seeds, sugar, onion, paprika, vinegars and vegetable oil.

5. Add dressing to taste and gently toss the salad. Makes 8 servings.

Brands may vary by region; substitute a similar product.

BOSKOVICH
FARMS, INCORPORATED

Apple-Crab Salad
YAKIMA-ROCHE FRUIT ▲

1 pound fresh crabmeat
1 large Washington apple (variety of choice), cored and thinly sliced
1 cup whole pecans
1 cup red seedless grapes
Gorgonzola cheese, crumbled, to taste
3/4 cup mayonnaise
1 cup sour cream
Red lettuce
Thin slice of lemon, for garnish
Parsley sprig, for garnish

1. Combine crabmeat, apple, pecans, grapes and Gorgonzola in a bowl.

2. Combine mayonnaise and sour cream in a large bowl. Stir in crab mixture. Chill for at least 2 hours before serving.

3. Serve on a bed of red lettuce, garnished with a lemon slice and a sprig of parsley. Makes 6-8 servings.

YAKIMA-ROCHE FRUIT SALES, L.L.C.

Greens with Cherry Vinaigrette
PRIMAVERA ▼

2 tablespoons butter
2 tablespoons sugar
1/2 cup walnuts
4 cups fresh spring greens
1/4 cup thinly sliced red onion
3/4 cup cubed Crystal Market*
   Granny Smith apple
1 cup Prima Frutta* fresh cherries,
   pitted and halved

CHERRY VINAIGRETTE
1/4 cup chopped fresh parsley
1 tablespoon minced shallot
1/2 tablespoon honey
1/2 teaspoon ground white pepper
2 tablespoons white wine
   (sweet or dry)
3/4 cup white balsamic vinegar
1/2 cup Prima Frutta* fresh
   cherries, pitted, diced, juiced
   and strained (discard skins)
1 cup olive oil

1. Prepare Cherry Vinaigrette: Combine parsley, shallot, honey, pepper, wine, vinegar and cherry juice. Slowly whisk in olive oil. Cover and refrigerate overnight.

2. Melt butter and sugar in a small saucepan over medium heat. Toss in walnuts and cook until coated and slightly darkened. Set aside.

3. Place greens in a salad bowl and toss with 1/2 cup vinaigrette until lightly coated. Add onion, apples, cherries and walnuts. Makes 4 servings.

Brands may vary by region; substitute a similar product.

Asian Pear and Pluot Salad
KINGSBURG ORCHARDS ▲

1 tablespoon Asian sesame oil

3 tablespoons vegetable oil

1 tablespoon toasted sesame seeds

4 tablespoons seasoned rice vinegar

5 teaspoons soy sauce

1/4 teaspoon Dijon mustard

1/8 teaspoon salt (optional)

1 large Kingsburg Orchards Asian pear, cored and thinly sliced

2 Dinosaur Brand pluots, pitted and thinly sliced

10 cups mixed salad greens

2 green onions, finely chopped

3 tablespoons chopped fresh cilantro

1/4 cup slivered almonds, toasted

1/3 cup crispy chow mein noodles

1. Combine sesame oil, vegetable oil, sesame seeds, rice vinegar, soy sauce, mustard and salt in a small bowl and whisk together. May be prepared ahead and refrigerated.

2. In a large bowl, combine remaining ingredients.

3. Whisk the dressing well, pour over the salad mixture, toss and serve. Makes 6-8 servings.

Southwest Chicken and Pear Salad
ALL STATE PACKERS/
ASSOCIATED FRUIT ▲

3 Bartlett or Bosc pears, cored and sliced

3 tablespoons lemon juice

Lettuce leaves

12 ounces cooked chicken, thinly sliced

1 medium tomato, seeded and diced

1 cup seeded and diced cucumber

1/4 cup chopped green chiles

1/4 cup chopped onion

1 small garlic clove, minced

2 tablespoons chopped fresh cilantro, plus leaves for garnish

2 tablespoons olive oil

Salt and pepper

1. Dip pears in lemon juice; arrange on lettuce leaves with chicken slices.

2. In a bowl, combine tomato, cucumber, chiles, onion, garlic, chopped cilantro, olive oil, and salt and pepper to taste. Spoon over pears and chicken.

3. Garnish with cilantro leaves. Makes 4 servings.

Festive Party Salad
DOLE ▼

4 cups (1 pound) Dole* Fresh Frozen Mixed Fruit,
   partially thawed

12 cups (1 pound) lightly packed Dole* Chopped Hearts of Romaine
   Salad Blend

2 cups chopped fresh Dole* Tropical Gold Pineapple *or* 2 cups canned
   Dole* Pineapple Chunks, drained

1/3 cup prepared raspberry vinaigrette

3 ripe Dole* Bananas, divided

1 cup Dole* Green Grapes

1. Combine mixed fruit, salad greens and pineapple in a large salad bowl.

2. Place vinaigrette and 1 chopped banana in a blender or a food processor container and blend until smooth.

3. Slice 2 bananas into 1/2-inch-thick pieces and add to the salad just before serving.

4. Toss salad with dressing and garnish with grapes. Makes 10-12 servings.

* Brands may vary by region; substitute a similar product.

Cara Cara Orange Spinach Salad
BEE SWEET CITRUS ▲

4 cups spinach, washed and dried well

2 cups bite-size pieces romaine lettuce

5 strawberries, hulled and sliced

1 1/2 Bee Sweet* Cara Cara oranges

1/4 cup crumbled blue cheese

VINAIGRETTE

3 tablespoons balsamic vinegar

1/4 teaspoon salt

1/4 teaspoon freshly ground black pepper

1/2 cup olive oil

1. Place greens in a salad bowl. Add sliced strawberries.

2. Remove peel from the whole orange, slice orange into rounds and cut rounds in half. Add to greens and strawberries.

3. Squeeze the juice of the 1/2 orange over all ingredients in the bowl.

4. Sprinkle blue cheese over the salad.

5. To prepare the vinaigrette, whisk together vinegar, salt and pepper in a small bowl. Gradually whisk in olive oil until emulsified.

6. Toss salad with enough vinaigrette to moisten. Serve immediately. Makes 4-6 servings.

Tip: Bee Sweet Citrus navel or Valencia oranges can be substituted for Cara Cara oranges.

* Brands may vary by region; substitute a similar product.

White Nectarine Salad
with Raspberry Vinaigrette
TRINITY FRUIT ▲

RASPBERRY VINAIGRETTE

1/2 cup raspberry vinegar

3 tablespoons lemon juice

1 medium shallot, coarsely chopped

2 tablespoons granulated sugar

2/3 cup canola oil

Kosher salt

Freshly ground black pepper

2 Trinity white nectarines

1 tablespoon lemon juice

12 or more butter lettuce leaves, washed and dried

1/2 cup raspberries

1/2 cup pecan halves, lightly toasted

1/2 cup crumbled goat cheese

Kosher salt

Freshly ground black pepper

1. Prepare Raspberry Vinaigrette: In a food processor fitted with the steel blade, process vinegar, lemon juice, shallot and sugar for 5 seconds. Add oil in a thin stream. Season to taste with salt and pepper.

2. Slice nectarines and toss gently with lemon juice.

3. Divide lettuce leaves among 4 chilled salad plates. Arrange nectarines, raspberries and pecans artfully on lettuce leaves. Garnish with crumbled goat cheese and drizzle with vinaigrette. Sprinkle with salt and pepper just before serving. Makes 4 servings.

Recipe created by Roy Harland, executive chef/partner,
Slates Restaurant, Fresno, California.

Tropical Martini Fruit Salad
BOUNTY FRESH/LEGEND PRODUCE/ BANANERA DEL CARIBE ▲

1 cup sugar
1 cup water
1/4 teaspoon cayenne pepper
1 stick cinnamon
2 tablespoons freshly squeezed lime juice
1 whole mango, diced
1 cup diced cantaloupe
1 cup diced pineapple
2 tablespoons freshly chopped mint
2 tablespoons chopped dry-roasted peanuts

1. In a small pan, stir sugar into water. Bring to a boil, lower heat and simmer for 2 minutes. Add cayenne and cinnamon and remove pan from the heat. Let cool and add lime juice.

2. In a medium bowl, combine mango, cantaloupe and pineapple.

3. Remove cinnamon stick from the cooled syrup and pour over the fruit. Cover and refrigerate for 1 hour.

4. Stir chopped mint into the fruit. Spoon the fruit into 6 large chilled martini glasses. Garnish with peanuts. Makes 6 servings.

Recipe courtesy of Chef Allen Susser.

Orange, Avocado and Black Olive Salad
OUTSPAN ▲

1/3 cup buttermilk
2 tablespoons olive oil
1 tablespoon red wine vinegar
1 tablespoon honey mustard
1 teaspoon grated orange peel
Salt and pepper
8 cups mixed salad greens, including radicchio, watercress and arugula
3 Outspan* oranges, peeled and sectioned
1 Hass avocado, peeled and cut into lengthwise slices
1/2 cup pitted large black olives, sliced
1/2 small red onion, halved lengthwise and cut into thin strips
2 tablespoons chopped fresh parsley

1. In a bowl, whisk together buttermilk, olive oil, vinegar, mustard and grated orange peel until smooth; season to taste with salt and pepper. Cover and refrigerate.

2. Line a wide, shallow serving bowl with salad greens. Top with drained orange sections and avocado slices. Sprinkle with sliced olives, onion and parsley.

3. Drizzle dressing over salad just before serving. Makes 6 servings.

* Brands may vary by region; substitute a similar product.

Avocado Fruit Stand Salad
HASS AVOCADO ▼

1 pound European-style prepackaged salad, any variety

3 kiwis, peeled, cut in half lengthwise and sliced in half rounds

2 red or pink grapefruit, peeled
and segmented

2 cups sliced strawberries

2 large fresh ripe Hass avocados,
peeled, one cut into cubes, the
other sliced into 8 portions

DRESSING

1/3 cup olive oil

3 tablespoons raspberry vinegar

3 tablespoons chopped walnuts,
toasted

2 teaspoons grated lime peel

2 tablespoons fresh lime juice

2 tablespoons chopped fresh basil

1/2 teaspoon dry mustard

1/2 teaspoon salt

1/4 teaspoon ground black pepper

1. To prepare the dressing, whisk together all ingredients in a small bowl;
set aside.

2. In a large salad bowl, combine salad mix, kiwis, grapefruit, strawberries
and cubed avocado.

3. Just before serving, whisk together dressing and pour over salad.
Toss salad to coat with dressing. Arrange avocado slices on top.
Makes 4-6 servings.

*Presented by Hass Avocado Board, Calavo Growers, Index Fresh, West Pak Avocado, McDaniel Fruit,
Giumarra, Del Rey Avocado and Mission Produce.*

Pasta, Avocado and Bell Pepper with Feta Cheese Salad
HASS AVOCADO ▼

8 ounces penne or other short macaroni-style pasta
1/2 cup prepared vinaigrette
3/4 cup diced red bell pepper
3/4 cup diced green bell pepper
3/4 cup crumbled feta cheese
1/2 cup chopped onion
1/3 cup chopped black olives
3 tablespoons chopped fresh parsley
1 garlic clove, finely chopped
2 large fresh Hass avocados
1 tablespoon lemon juice

1. Cook pasta in salted boiling water until just tender, about 10 minutes; drain well. Place warm pasta in a bowl and toss with vinaigrette; let cool.

2. Fold in bell pepper, feta, onion, olives, parsley and garlic. Chill.

3. Bring salad to room temperature before serving.

4. Cut avocados into chunks; gently toss with lemon juice. Fold avocado into salad. Makes 6 servings.

Presented by Hass Avocado Board, Calavo Growers, Index Fresh, West Pak Avocado, McDaniel Fruit, Giumarra, Del Rey Avocado and Mission Produce.

Mango and Avocado Salad
FRESKA PRODUCE ▲

1 large hothouse cucumber, peeled, sliced lengthwise, seeded and cut into 1/4-inch crosswise slices
1 cup cherry tomatoes, halved
1/2 cup cooked green beans, thinly sliced
1/2 cup fresh bean sprouts
1/3 cup rice vinegar
2 tablespoons freshly squeezed lime juice
2 red Thai chiles, seeded and minced
2 teaspoons sugar
1 avocado, peeled, pitted and sliced
1 ripe Freska mango, peeled, pitted and sliced
1/4 cup fresh mint leaves, slivered, for garnish

1. Place cucumber, tomatoes, green beans and bean sprouts in a bowl and toss to combine. Cover and refrigerate for at least 1 hour and up to 4 hours.

2. Combine vinegar, lime juice, chiles and sugar in a bowl. Stir until sugar dissolves.

3. To serve, arrange salad mixture, avocado and mango on 4 plates. Drizzle with dressing and garnish with mint. Makes 4 servings.

Grape Tomato and Avocado Salad
NATURESWEET ▲

3 tablespoons olive oil
1 1/2 teaspoons white vinegar
Kosher salt
Freshly ground black pepper
2 ripe avocados, peeled, pitted and cut into chunks
12 ounces NatureSweet* grape tomatoes, halved
1/4 cup very thinly sliced red onion
Leaves of 1 sprig fresh thyme

1. Whisk together olive oil and vinegar in a salad bowl. Add salt and pepper to taste.

2. Put the remaining ingredients in the bowl. Toss to combine. Season again to taste. Makes 2-4 servings.

Brands may vary by region; substitute a similar product.

Spring Mix with Artichoke Hearts and Roasted Garlic
EARTHBOUND FARM

10 garlic cloves, peeled
1/2 cup olive oil
1/4 cup lemon juice
3 tablespoons chopped fresh parsley
1 tablespoon dried oregano
1 teaspoon salt
1/2 cup thinly sliced green onions
1 13-ounce can artichoke hearts, drained and rinsed, cut in quarters
3 Roma tomatoes, diced
2 cups small white mushrooms, cut in quarters
8 ounces Earthbound Farm* Spring Mix

1. Preheat oven to 350°F.
2. Place garlic cloves and olive oil in a small ovenproof pan. Cover with foil. Roast for 30 minutes, or until garlic is light golden brown. Remove foil and let cool to room temperature. In a small bowl, mash roasted garlic with a fork, then whisk in lemon juice, parsley, oregano and salt.
3. Combine green onions, artichokes, tomatoes and mushrooms in a bowl and toss with half of the roasted garlic vinaigrette. Let stand for 1 hour.
4. Place spring mix in a salad bowl and toss with remaining vinaigrette. Add marinated vegetables. Serve immediately. Makes 4 servings.

Brands may vary by region; substitute a similar product.

Layered Salad with Hearts of Romaine
ANDY BOY

2 heads Andy Boy* romaine hearts, shredded
2 carrots, sliced
2 celery ribs, sliced
1 red bell pepper, sliced
1/2 medium red onion, sliced
8 ounces frozen peas
1 cup mayonnaise
1 tablespoon sugar
1/2 cup grated Cheddar cheese
2 strips bacon, cooked crisp and crumbled

1. Place shredded romaine in a large bowl.
2. Layer the remaining ingredients on the romaine in the following order: carrots, celery, bell pepper, onion and peas.
3. Combine mayonnaise and sugar. Cover the frozen peas with a thin layer of mayonnaise mixture. Top with Cheddar and bacon.
4. Refrigerate from 1 hour to overnight. Before serving, toss all the ingredients. Makes 8-10 servings.

Brands may vary by region; substitute a similar product.

Spring Mix Salad with Feta, Pecans and Strawberry Vinaigrette
BABÉ FARMS ▲

1 1-pound basket ripe strawberries, hulled and halved
8 cups Babé Farms* Spring Mix
1 7-ounce package crumbled feta cheese (about 1 1/3 cups)
1/2 cup pecans, toasted
1/2 cup olive oil
3 tablespoons balsamic vinegar
1 tablespoon sugar
Salt and pepper

1. Mash enough of the strawberries to measure 1/3 cup.

2. Place remaining strawberries in a large bowl. Add Spring Mix, feta and pecans.

3. Place oil, vinegar and sugar in a small bowl and whisk to blend. Whisk in mashed strawberries. Season with salt and pepper to taste.

4. Add vinaigrette to salad and toss to coat. Serve immediately. Makes 6 servings.

Brands may vary by region; substitute a similar product.

Western Bean Salad
HORMEL ▲

SALAD
1 15-ounce can pinto beans, drained and rinsed
1 15-ounce can garbanzo beans, drained
2 cups cherry tomato halves
1 cup Chi-Chi's* salsa
2 ounces Hormel* pepperoni, diced
3 ounces Hormel/Kirkland Signature* Precooked Bacon, crumbled, or Hormel* Crumbled Bacon
1 small red onion, cut in 1/4-inch slices
Lettuce leaves

DRESSING
1/4 cup vegetable oil
2 tablespoons white wine vinegar
1 teaspoon sugar
3/4 teaspoon chili powder
1/4 teaspoon coarsely ground pepper
1/4 teaspoon salt

1. In a large bowl, combine all salad ingredients except lettuce leaves. Mix well and set aside.

2. In a small bowl, combine all dressing ingredients and mix well.

3. Toss dressing with the salad. Cover and refrigerate for 1 hour to let flavors blend.

4. Serve on lettuce leaves. Makes 6-8 servings.

Brands may vary by region; substitute a similar product.

Chinese Noodle and Vegetable Salad
FOXY FOODS ▲

DRESSING

¹/₄ cup olive oil or vegetable oil

¹/₄ cup white wine vinegar

1 tablespoon Asian sesame oil

1 tablespoon soy sauce

1 tablespoon fresh lemon juice

1 tablespoon ketchup

³/₄ teaspoon salt

¹/₄ teaspoon grated fresh ginger

¹/₄ teaspoon sugar

¹/₈ teaspoon freshly ground
   black pepper

SALAD

1 head Foxy* iceberg lettuce,
   shredded, *or* 1 bunch Foxy*
   romaine hearts, torn into
   bite-size pieces

3 cups Foxy* broccoli florets
   (1 bunch)

¹/₄ cup sliced mushrooms

¹/₄ cup bias-sliced celery

¹/₄ cup shredded carrot

¹/₄ cup chopped red or green
   bell pepper

1 cup crisp chow mein noodles

1. To prepare dressing, place all ingredients in a food processor or blender. Cover and process until well blended. Set aside.

2. In a large bowl, toss together lettuce, broccoli, mushrooms, celery, carrot and bell pepper. Drizzle dressing over salad and toss well to coat.

3. Spoon salad onto 4 plates. Sprinkle with chow mein noodles. Makes 4 servings.

* Brands may vary by region; substitute a similar product.

Campari Tomato and Mango Slaw
EUROFRESH FARMS ▲

8-10 Eurofresh Farms Campari tomatoes, cut into ¹/₄-inch strips

2 mangoes, ripe but still a little firm, peeled, sliced thin and cut into
   fine julienne strips*

1 bunch fresh cilantro, chopped

¹/₂ cup raspberry vinegar

¹/₈ teaspoon seeded and very finely chopped habanero pepper

1. Place all ingredients in a stainless steel bowl and toss lightly, being careful not to mash the tomatoes.

2. Marinate for 1 hour before serving. Makes 6-8 servings.

* If the mango isn't sweet, add a sprinkle of sugar while tossing.

EURO
FRESH
FARMS
GARDEN FRESH FLAVOR

Potato Salad
TOP BRASS ▲

4 strips bacon
1 pound Top Brass* small red potatoes
1 teaspoon salt, divided
¹/₂ cup mayonnaise
1 teaspoon Dijon mustard
¹/₂ teaspoon freshly ground pepper
2 green onions, sliced
1 hard-boiled egg, chopped

1. Cook bacon until crispy. Drain, reserving a tablespoon of the fat. Crumble bacon and set aside.

2. Place potatoes in a large saucepan. Cover with cold water. Add a tablespoon of bacon fat and ¹/₂ teaspoon salt. Bring to a boil on medium-high heat and cook until potatoes are tender, 15-20 minutes. Drain and let potatoes cool, then cut into bite-size pieces.

3. In a small bowl, mix mayonnaise, mustard, ¹/₂ teaspoon salt and pepper.

4. Place potatoes, green onions and egg in a bowl and toss with dressing. Add bacon. Serve chilled. Makes 4 servings.

* Brands may vary by region; substitute a similar product.

Turkey and Jarlsberg Flatbread Rollers
BLT and Jarlsberg Flatbread Rollers
COSTCO DELI AND BAKERY ▲

Convenience and quality all wrapped into one—Costco Deli's ready-made Turkey and Jarlsberg or Bacon, Lettuce, Tomato and Jarlsberg Lahvash Flatbread Rollers give you a gourmet sandwich shop experience. Jarlsberg cheese is all natural, with a distinctive mellow, nutty flavor and creamy texture that is delicious in sandwiches made with Damascus Bakeries Fat Free Lahvash Flatbread.

For a healthy, light meal try Jarlsberg Sunset Salad with Damascus Bakeries' "Nutritious & Delicious" Roll-Ups (found in most Costco Bakery sections).

JARLSBERG SUNSET SALAD
1 large cucumber
2 large ripe tomatoes, sliced
2 green onions with tops, sliced
1 cup (4 ounces) diced Jarlsberg or Jarlsberg Lite cheese
2 tablespoons chopped fresh basil
¹/₂ cup chopped walnuts
Prepared vinaigrette

1. Halve cucumber lengthwise. Scrape out seeds with a spoon and slice into half-moons.

2. In a large bowl, combine cucumber, tomatoes, green onions, cheese, basil and walnuts. Toss with vinaigrette to taste. Makes 4 servings.

Normandy Blend Salad
NUTRIVERDE ▼

2 cups Kirkland Signature Normandy Blend frozen vegetables

Yolks from 2 soft-boiled eggs

$1/2$ cup balsamic vinegar

$1/2$ cup olive oil

Salt and pepper

$1/2$ cup halved seedless white grapes

$1/2$ cup halved seedless red grapes

2 Granny Smith or other tart apples, cored and sliced

$1/2$ head iceberg lettuce

1. Heat frozen vegetables in a microwave at 50% power (defrost) for 1 $1/2$-2 minutes. Drain well and refrigerate until ready to use.

2. In a bowl, whisk together soft-boiled egg yolks, vinegar, olive oil, and salt and pepper to taste. Use immediately or cover and refrigerate.

3. Combine chilled vegetables, grapes and apples in a bowl. Add dressing and toss well.

4. Place a layer of lettuce on each of 4 plates and top with the salad. Makes 4 servings.

Broccoli with Maple-Sesame Dressing
EAT SMART ▼

3 tablespoons maple syrup
2 tablespoons rice vinegar
1 tablespoon toasted sesame seeds
1 teaspoon chopped fresh cilantro
$1/4$ teaspoon ground cumin
Salt and pepper
2 tablespoons olive oil
1 tablespoon Asian sesame oil
3 cups Eat Smart* broccoli cut into bite-size pieces
1 cup sweet onion cut into wedges
1 cup red bell pepper cut into wedges

1. In a small bowl, combine maple syrup, rice vinegar, sesame seeds, cilantro, cumin, and salt and pepper to taste. Set aside to let flavors blend.
2. Heat olive oil and sesame oil in a large frying pan over medium heat. Add broccoli, onion and bell pepper; cook until crisp-tender.
3. Place vegetables in a serving dish. Drizzle with dressing.
Makes 4 servings.

Brands may vary by region; substitute a similar product.

Gazpacho de Almejas (Clams)
SEA WATCH ▲

1 51-ounce can Sea Watch* Chopped Clams, including liquid

1 46-ounce can tomato juice

1 15-ounce can diced tomatoes

1 4-ounce can chopped green chiles

1 cup ketchup

1 small sweet onion, diced

1 small bunch celery, chopped

2 cucumbers, chopped

Juice of 3 limes

4 avocados, diced

1 teaspoon ground black pepper

1 teaspoon ground cumin

Hot sauce to taste

1. Combine all ingredients in a large bowl; the juice from the clams is essential to the flavor of this recipe.

2. Chill for at least 1 hour before serving. It is even better the next day. Makes 10-12 servings.

* Brands may vary by region; substitute a similar product.

Gazpacho
WILSONBATIZ ▲

2 large Royal Flavor* hothouse-grown beefsteak tomatoes

4 small zucchini or yellow summer squash

1 carrot, peeled

1 Royal Flavor* hothouse-grown seedless cucumber, skinned

1/4 cup chopped onion

1 Royal Flavor* hothouse-grown red bell pepper, cored and seeded

3 garlic cloves, peeled

1/4 cup fresh lime juice

2 tablespoons olive oil

1/4 cup chopped fresh herbs (cilantro, mint, dill, etc.)

2 teaspoons chopped fresh jalapeño pepper

1 tablespoon red wine vinegar

6-8 ounces tomato juice or V8 juice (can use Spicy)

Salt and cracked pepper to taste

GARNISH

Rosemary sprigs, red bell pepper slices

1. Puree all the ingredients together.

2. Fill bowls with gazpacho, and garnish with rosemary sprigs and slices of red bell pepper. Makes 8 servings.

* Brands may vary by region; substitute a similar product.

WILSONBATIZ.

Fiery Gazpacho
THE OPPENHEIMER GROUP/
WINDSET FARMS ▲

2 cups seeded and diced
   Windset Farms* Campari
   or Oppenheimer*
   Beefsteak tomato
$^{1}/_{2}$ cup diced yellow bell pepper
1 cup diced English cucumber
$^{1}/_{2}$ cup diced red onion
1 cup vegetable broth
$^{1}/_{4}$-$^{1}/_{2}$ cup extra-virgin olive oil
Juice of $^{1}/_{2}$ lemon
2 tablespoons balsamic vinegar
$^{1}/_{4}$ cup minced fresh parsley

1 tablespoon minced fresh
   oregano or 1 teaspoon dried
2 tablespoons Worcestershire
   sauce
2 large garlic cloves, minced
Dash of sea salt
1 hard-boiled egg
5 $^{1}/_{4}$ cups tomato juice
$^{1}/_{2}$ cup dry bread crumbs
Freshly ground black pepper
Hot pepper sauce
Sour cream

1. Combine vegetables in a large bowl. Gently stir in broth, oil, lemon juice, vinegar, parsley, oregano and Worcestershire sauce.

2. Place garlic, sea salt and egg in a small bowl; mash with a fork until blended.

3. Stir tomato juice and egg mixture into vegetable mixture. Stir in bread crumbs until dissolved. Add salt, pepper and hot pepper sauce to taste. Refrigerate overnight.

4. Serve with dollops of sour cream. Makes 12 servings.

Brands may vary by region; substitute a similar product.

expect the world from us

Slow-Cooker Potato Soup
RUSSET POTATO EXCHANGE/
ALSUM PRODUCE/ANTHONY FARMS ▲

4 Wisconsin Premium* russet potatoes, peeled and cut into
   small pieces
2 leeks, coarsely chopped
2 onions, coarsely chopped
3 ribs celery, coarsely chopped
4 chicken bouillon cubes
1 10 $^{3}/_{4}$-ounce can cream of mushroom soup
1 10 $^{3}/_{4}$-ounce can cream of celery soup
1 tablespoon dried parsley flakes
4 cups water
1 $^{1}/_{2}$ teaspoons salt
2 tablespoons margarine or butter
1 12-ounce can evaporated milk
Chopped chives, for garnish

1. Place all ingredients except evaporated milk and chives in a slow cooker. Cover and cook on low for 10-12 hours or on high for 5 hours.

2. Stir in evaporated milk during the last hour, and cook until the vegetables are tender.

3. Garnish each serving with chives. Makes 8 servings.

Brands may vary by region; substitute a similar product.

Minestrone alla Fiorentina with Meat Lasagna
KIRKLAND SIGNATURE ▼

Kirkland Signature Meat Lasagne
1/4 cup Kirkland Signature extra-virgin olive oil
1 large yellow onion, thinly sliced
1/2 cup finely chopped ham
1 small head savoy cabbage, shredded
2 ribs celery, finely chopped
2 garlic cloves, minced
1 sprig fresh rosemary
2 sprigs fresh thyme
1 15 1/2-ounce can cannellini beans

3 quarts vegetable broth
1/2 teaspoon cracked black pepper
Parmigiano-Reggiano cheese

1. Prepare lasagna according to package directions.

2. To prepare soup: Heat oil in a large soup pot over medium heat. Add onion, ham, cabbage, celery and garlic; sauté until the vegetables are tender.

3. Add rosemary, thyme, beans, vegetable broth and pepper. Simmer for 1 hour. Taste and adjust seasoning as necessary.

4. Serve in soup bowls with grated Parmigiano-Reggiano cheese.

Makes 12 servings.

Tip: Add fresh rolls or baguettes from the Costco Bakery to complete this delicious and easy-to-prepare meal.

KIRKLAND *Signature*

Spinach, Celery, Sausage and Pasta Soup
METZ FRESH ▲

16 ounces any kind of sausage links

4 cups chicken broth

2 14 1/2-ounce cans diced tomatoes with basil, garlic and oregano

2 cups thinly sliced celery hearts with leaves

1 cup uncooked small shell pasta

Salt and pepper

4 cups Metz Fresh Cello* bagged spinach leaves

4 tablespoons freshly grated Parmesan cheese

2 tablespoons chopped fresh basil (optional)

1. Heat a large saucepan or soup pot over medium heat. Remove casings from sausage, add sausage to the pan and cook, stirring to crumble, for 10 minutes, or until browned. Drain and return sausage to the pan.

2. Add broth, tomatoes, celery, pasta, and salt and pepper to taste to the pan; bring to a boil over high heat. Cover, reduce heat and simmer for 20 minutes, or until pasta is done.

3. Remove from heat and stir in spinach until wilted. Sprinkle each serving with cheese and basil, if desired. Serve with hot Italian bread. Makes 8 servings.

Brands may vary by region; substitute a similar product.

Soup di Napoli
CLASSICO ▲

8 ounces small pasta shells

1/2 pound Italian sausage links, sliced

1 small zucchini, sliced (about 1 cup)

1 small summer squash, sliced (about 1 cup)

1/2 cup chopped onion

3 cups water

1 32-ounce jar Classico* di Napoli (Tomato and Basil) Pasta Sauce

1 tablespoon beef-flavor instant bouillon

1. Cook pasta shells according to package directions; drain.

2. In a large pot, brown sausage over medium-high heat.

3. Stir in zucchini, summer squash and onion; cook until tender.

4. Add water, pasta sauce and bouillon; bring to a boil. Reduce heat, cover and simmer for 15 minutes.

5. Stir in pasta shells. Makes 6-8 servings.

Brands may vary by region; substitute a similar product.

Italian Sausage and Spicy Black Bean Soup
PREMIO ▼

3 tablespoons olive oil

1 medium onion, chopped

3 garlic cloves, minced

1 medium green bell pepper, chopped

2 teaspoons ground cumin

Salt and pepper

8 links Premio* Hot or Sweet Italian Sausage, cooked according to package directions, cut lengthwise and sliced

6-8 cups chicken or vegetable broth

2 15-ounce cans black beans, rinsed and drained

1. In a large saucepan or soup pot, combine olive oil, onion, garlic, bell pepper and cumin. Cook over low heat until soft. Season to taste with salt and pepper.

2. Increase heat to medium and add sausage, stirring to combine well. Cook for 5-8 minutes, or until it begins to stick to the pan.

3. Add chicken broth and beans. Bring to a simmer, stirring to prevent sticking. Simmer, uncovered, for 20-30 minutes, adding water or broth if needed. Check seasoning and partially mash beans with a potato masher to thicken the soup. Makes 8-10 servings.

Brands may vary by region; substitute a similar product.

Side Dishes

Crab-Stuffed Twice-Baked Potatoes
CONAGRA ◀

4 medium baking potatoes
¹/₂ cup milk
¹/₂ cup butter
1 teaspoon salt
2 tablespoons grated onion
1 pound ConAgra king crab meat, shredded
Sharp Cheddar cheese, grated

1. Preheat oven to 450°F.
2. Bake potatoes for 1 hour, or until tender. Remove from the oven and let cool.
3. Cut potatoes in half lengthwise. Scoop flesh into a bowl; save skins.
4. Add milk, butter, salt and onion to potato flesh. Beat with a hand mixer until creamy.
5. Fold in crab. Spoon mixture into the potato skins. Top with grated cheese.
6. Place stuffed potatoes in a baking pan. Bake for 15-20 minutes, or until heated through. Makes 4 servings.

Easy Cheesy Potatoes
KRAFT ▲

Cooking spray
4 medium potatoes, unpeeled, quartered and cut into ¹/₂-inch chunks (about 4 cups)
¹/₂ pound Velveeta Pasteurized Prepared Cheese Product, cubed
¹/₂ medium onion, chopped (about ¹/₂ cup)
¹/₄ cup Kraft Mayo Real Mayonnaise or Miracle Whip Dressing
4 slices Oscar Mayer* bacon, cooked, drained and crumbled (about ¹/₄ cup)

1. Preheat oven to 400°F. Coat an 8-inch square baking dish with cooking spray.
2. Place potatoes, Velveeta, onion and mayonnaise in the baking dish and stir to combine. Sprinkle with bacon.
3. Bake for 40-45 minutes, or until potatoes are tender.
Makes 10 servings.

Brands may vary by region; substitute a similar product.

Cheddar, Corn and Salsa Mashed Spuds
BASIN GOLD ▲

2 1/2 pounds (about 3 very large) Basin Gold* russet potatoes, peeled and cut in half
1/4 cup milk or half-and-half
6 tablespoons butter
1/2 teaspoon salt
1/2 cup salsa
1/2 cup corn kernels
1 cup shredded Cheddar cheese
Thinly sliced green onions, for garnish

1. Place potatoes in a large pot and cover with water. Bring to a boil, then reduce heat to low and cook until tender, about 20 minutes.

2. Meanwhile, place milk, butter and salt in a saucepan. Bring just to a simmer over low heat—do not boil. Remove from heat and stir in salsa and corn.

3. When potatoes are cooked, drain well, then return them to the pot. Shake the pot over low heat for about 30 seconds to dry them out.

4. Remove potatoes from heat and add the hot milk mixture. Mash the potatoes until they are fluffy. Fold in cheese. Sprinkle with green onions. Makes 6 servings.

Recipe created by Kathy Casey Food Studios.
* Brands may vary by region; substitute a similar product.

Flying Fish Potato-Peanut Cakes
WALLACE FARMS POTATOES/SKAGIT VALLEY'S BEST PRODUCE/VALLEY PRIDE ▲

3/4 pound Washington Yukon Gold potatoes
1 slice bacon
1 cup cooked fresh corn kernels (about 2 ears)
1/4 cup finely chopped onion
1/4 cup finely chopped red bell pepper
1 teaspoon chopped fresh thyme
1/4 cup sliced green onions
1/4 cup chopped peanuts
1/2 teaspoon salt
1 large egg, lightly beaten
Nonstick cooking spray
Fresh thyme, for garnish (optional)

1. Place potatoes in a saucepan; cover with water. Bring to a boil, reduce heat and simmer until tender. Drain and cool. Peel and shred potatoes into a large bowl.

2. Fry bacon in a large nonstick skillet over medium heat until crisp. Remove from pan, let cool, then crumble. Add corn, onion, bell pepper and thyme to drippings in pan; cook until onion is tender.

3. Combine potatoes, bacon, corn mixture, green onions, peanuts, salt and egg; stir with a fork until well mixed.

4. Coat a nonstick griddle or large skillet with cooking spray. For each cake, spoon about 1/3 cup potato mixture onto the hot griddle or skillet; flatten slightly with a spatula. Cook for 5 minutes, or until golden brown on each side.

5. Garnish with thyme, if desired. Makes 8 servings.

Recipe provided by Chef Christine Keff, Flying Fish restaurant, Seattle.

Cheesy Ranch Potato Casserole
MACK FARMS/SOUTH FLORIDA POTATO GROWERS EXCHANGE ▲

10-12 red new potatoes
¹/₄ teaspoon salt
Cooking spray
Prepared ranch dressing
2 cups shredded Cheddar cheese
4 strips bacon, cooked and crumbled

1. Preheat oven to 400°F.
2. Place potatoes and salt in a large pot and cover with water. Bring to a boil, then lower heat and simmer just until tender. Do not overcook.
3. Spray a 9-by-13-inch casserole with cooking spray. Coat the bottom of the casserole thoroughly with ranch dressing.
4. Drain potatoes and transfer to the casserole. Top potatoes with cheese and bacon.
5. Bake for approximately 20 minutes, or until thoroughly heated. Makes 6 servings.

Spinach and Potatoes au Gratin
NEWSTAR ▲

2 tablespoons butter
2 tablespoons flour
1 ¹/₂ cups milk
1 ¹/₂ cups shredded Cheddar cheese, divided
8 strips bacon
1 cup chopped onions
16 ounces NewStar* spinach
6-8 medium red or gold potatoes, sliced ¹/₄ inch thick
1 teaspoon salt
1 teaspoon pepper

1. Preheat oven to 400°F.
2. Melt butter in a saucepan over medium-low heat. Stir in flour until a paste forms. Slowly whisk in milk; bring to a simmer. Add 1 ¹/₄ cups cheese and stir until cheese is melted.
3. In a 10-inch frying pan, cook bacon until crisp; drain and crumble.
4. Add onions to bacon drippings and sauté over medium heat until tender. Add spinach and sauté for 30 seconds.
5. Layer half of potatoes in a 9-by-13-inch pan; season with half of salt and pepper. Add half of spinach and onions. Reserve 2 tablespoons of bacon; sprinkle half of remaining bacon over spinach. Repeat layering. Pour cheese sauce over all.
6. Bake for 40-50 minutes. Top with remaining cheese and bacon; bake for 5-10 minutes, or until browned. Makes 8 servings.

* Brands may vary by region; substitute a similar product.

Side Dishes ▮

Oven-Roasted Stringless Sugar Snaps Parmigiano
MANN'S ▲

4 cups Mann's* Stringless Sugar Snap Peas
1 tablespoon extra-virgin olive oil
Pinch of salt
1/3 cup slivered Parmigiano-Reggiano cheese
   (cut from a 2-ounce piece)

1. Preheat oven to 450°F.

2. Spread sugar snaps in a 9-by-13-inch baking pan. Sprinkle with olive oil and salt. Toss to coat.

3. Roast for 10 minutes.

4. Remove from the oven and spread cheese evenly over the top. Return to the oven and roast until cheese melts, about 3 minutes. Serve immediately. Makes 4 servings.

Tip: Cut "curls" from a wedge of Parmigiano-Reggiano with a cheese plane or vegetable peeler, rather than cutting it into slivers. Either way, the cheese will melt over the peas, making an irresistible vegetable side dish.

Brands may vary by region; substitute a similar product.

Portabella Mushroom Salad and Red Chile Vinaigrette
MONTEREY MUSHROOMS ▲

3 tablespoons olive oil
1 20-ounce package Monterey*
   Portabella mushrooms,
   coarsely chopped
1 tablespoon chopped
   fresh cilantro
Salt and pepper
1 pound asparagus, grilled
8 ounces goat cheese

1/2 cup smoked almonds,
   coarsely crushed

RED CHILE VINAIGRETTE
2 tablespoons Dijon mustard
1 tablespoon dark chile powder
1/4 cup balsamic vinegar
1/2 cup olive oil
Salt

1. Make Red Chile Vinaigrette: Whisk together mustard, chile powder and vinegar. Slowly whisk in olive oil until emulsified. Season to taste with salt and set aside.

2. Heat 3 tablespoons olive oil in a large sauté pan over high heat. Cook mushrooms until completely softened. Add cilantro and season to taste with salt and pepper.

3. Toss grilled asparagus with a few tablespoons of the vinaigrette and salt and pepper to taste.

4. Arrange 1/4 of the mushrooms in the center of each plate and asparagus around them. Sprinkle goat cheese and crushed almonds on the rim of the plate. Drizzle with more vinaigrette. Makes 4 servings.

Recipe created by Chef Angelo Corvino, Monterey Mushrooms, Inc.
Brands may vary by region; substitute a similar product.

Cashew-Topped Asparagus
ANN'S HOUSE OF NUTS/ ORIGINAL NUT HOUSE ▼

1 bunch fresh asparagus
1 .90-ounce packet béarnaise sauce mix
1/4 cup butter
1 cup milk
1/2 cup Kirkland Signature Indian Cashews
1 teaspoon olive oil
1/4 teaspoon red pepper flakes
1/8 teaspoon chile powder

1. Wash asparagus and trim about 2 inches off the ends. Add 2 inches of water to a saucepan and bring to a boil. Place asparagus in a steamer over the boiling water and cook for 8-10 minutes, or until tender.

2. Prepare béarnaise sauce according to package directions, using butter and milk.

3. In a sauté pan, toast cashews over medium heat in olive oil and seasonings for about 1-2 minutes.

4. Arrange asparagus on a serving platter. Pour sauce over asparagus and sprinkle with cashews. Makes 4 servings.

KIRKLAND *Signature*

Artichokes with Ricotta and Basil
OCEAN MIST FARMS ▲

4 medium to large Ocean Mist Farms* artichokes
2 tablespoons lemon juice or white wine vinegar
1 cup ricotta cheese
1/2 cup shredded Parmesan cheese, divided
1 egg
1/4 cup chopped fresh basil or 1 tablespoon dried basil
1/4 teaspoon freshly ground pepper
Olive oil
Salt and pepper

1. Preheat oven to 375°F.
2. Rinse artichokes. Trim off ends of stems and top third of petals. Cut artichokes in half lengthwise. Arrange, cut side down, in a 9-by-13-by-2-inch baking dish. Add water to fill halfway and lemon juice or vinegar. Cover tightly with foil. Bake until a petal pulls off easily, about 30 minutes.
3. Combine ricotta, 1/4 cup Parmesan, egg, basil and 1/4 teaspoon pepper in a medium bowl.
4. When artichokes are done, pour off cooking liquid. Turn artichokes cut side up. Remove fuzzy center with a grapefruit spoon or melon baller and soft inner leaves and discard. Brush cut surfaces with olive oil and sprinkle with salt and pepper to taste.
5. Spoon ricotta mixture into artichoke halves. Sprinkle with remaining Parmesan. Return to oven until tops are lightly browned, about 15-20 minutes. Makes 4 servings.

Brands may vary by region; substitute a similar product.

Spinach Bake
SHIITAKE-YA ▲

6 strips bacon, cut into bite-size pieces
1 small onion, chopped
4 cups Shiitake-Ya* Dried Sliced Mushrooms, rehydrated
4 eggs
2 16-ounce packages frozen chopped spinach, thawed and squeezed dry
1/4 cup fine dry bread crumbs
1 10 3/4-ounce can condensed cream of mushroom soup
1/4 cup freshly grated Parmesan cheese, divided
1/4 teaspoon each pepper, dried basil and dried oregano

1. Preheat oven to 350°F.
2. In a skillet, sauté bacon, onion and shiitake mushrooms over medium heat, stirring, until bacon is cooked.
3. In a large bowl, beat eggs. Stir in mushroom mixture and all other ingredients except 2 tablespoons of the Parmesan. Turn into a well-greased 9-by-13-inch casserole. Sprinkle with remaining Parmesan.
4. Bake, uncovered, for 35 minutes, or until the edges are beginning to brown. Makes 8 servings.

Tip: This dish can also be served cold as an appetizer, cut into bite-size pieces.

Brands may vary by region; substitute a similar product.

Shiitake-Ya™

Italian French Bean Sauté
LOS ANGELES SALAD COMPANY ▼

4 tablespoons olive oil

2 tablespoons crushed garlic

1 pound Los Angeles Salad Company* French green beans, trimmed

6 tablespoons chicken broth

5 ripe Roma tomatoes, seeded and cut into ¹/₂- to ³/₄-inch cubes

1 teaspoon dried Italian seasoning

Salt

Freshly ground black pepper

6 basil leaves, slivered

¹/₄ cup grated Parmigiano-Reggiano cheese

1. Heat olive oil in a sauté pan over medium heat. Add garlic and cook, stirring, for 1 minute.

2. Add beans and cook, stirring, for 2 minutes, making sure the beans are well coated.

3. Add chicken broth and continue to cook and stir the beans for 2 minutes.

4. Stir in tomatoes and Italian seasoning; cook for 2-3 minutes. Beans should be crisp (al dente). Season to taste with salt and pepper.

5. One minute before beans are done, add basil and cheese. Serve immediately. Makes 4-6 servings.

Recipe created by Chef Sim.
* Brands may vary by region; substitute a similar product.

Peas Pilaf
DAAWAT BASMATI RICE ▲

2 cups Daawat* basmati rice
1 cup green peas, fresh or frozen
1/4 teaspoon salt
2 teaspoons butter
1 small (3-ounce) onion, sliced
2-3 tablespoons chopped cashews
2-3 tablespoons raisins
1-inch piece cinnamon stick
1 bay leaf
3 peppercorns

1. Wash rice 2-3 times in fresh water. Place rice in a bowl, cover with water and let soak for 30 minutes; drain.

2. Put 4 cups water in a heavy saucepan with a tight-fitting lid and bring to a boil. Add rice, green peas and salt. Reduce heat to low, cover and cook for 25 minutes, or until all the liquid is absorbed. Spread the rice in a flat dish or pan to cool and dry for 30 minutes.

3. Meanwhile, melt butter in a sauté pan over medium-high heat and fry onion until browned. Add cashews, raisins, cinnamon, bay leaf and peppercorns and fry for 1 minute.

4. Put the rice on a platter and garnish with the fried seasonings. Makes 4 servings.

* Brands may vary by region; substitute a similar product.

Pickled Pepper Relish
PRIME TIME INTERNATIONAL ▲

1/4 cup cider vinegar
3 tablespoons sugar
1/4 teaspoon mustard seed
1/4 teaspoon celery seed
1/4 teaspoon salt
Pinch of turmeric
1 medium Prime Time* red bell pepper, cut into 1/3-inch dice
1 medium Prime Time* green bell pepper, cut into 1/3-inch dice
1 large Vidalia or other sweet onion, cut into 1/3-inch dice

1. In a medium saucepan, combine vinegar, sugar, mustard seed, celery seed, salt and turmeric. Bring to a boil over medium-high heat.

2. Stir in bell peppers and onion. Simmer over medium-low heat, stirring occasionally, until peppers are tender and most of the liquid has evaporated, about 15 minutes.

3. Let cool. Serve with fish, hot dogs or hamburgers. Makes 6-8 servings.

Tip: This relish can be refrigerated for up to 1 week.

* Brands may vary by region; substitute a similar product.

Fiesta Rice Medley in Sweet Bell Peppers
SUNSET

1 tablespoon olive oil
1 onion, chopped
8 Sunset* Rainbow Sweet Bell Peppers: 2 chopped and 6 whole
1 16-ounce can corn kernels
1 1/4 cups Sunset* Salsa
1 cup chicken broth
1 1/2 cups instant rice
1/4 cup shredded Cheddar cheese
2 tablespoons grated Parmesan cheese

1. Preheat oven to 375°F.
2. Heat oil in a large pot over medium heat. Add onion and chopped peppers. Cook until tender.

3. Add corn, 1 cup salsa and chicken broth. Bring to a boil. Stir in rice, cover and reduce to low heat.
4. Slice 1/2 inch off tops of whole peppers and discard tops. Remove cores and seeds. Cut a thin slice from the bottom of each pepper.
5. Add Cheddar to the pot and fluff with the rice. Spoon rice into peppers.
6. Mix 1/4 cup salsa with 1/4 cup water; pour into a baking pan. Place stuffed peppers in the pan.
7. Bake for 20 minutes, or until tender. Sprinkle with Parmesan cheese. Makes 6 servings.

Brands may vary by region; substitute a similar product.

Chef's Choice

The world's best chefs have the special ability to infuse dishes with their unique personalities. We asked several top chefs to do their magic with the products supplied by these great companies:

Foster Farms *Bill & Cheryl Jamison*	**69**	
Swift *Susan Lamb Parenti*	**72**	
Tarantino *Leanne Ely*	**75**	
Gold Kist Farms *Mario Batali*	**78**	
Smithfield *Michael Brando*	**81**	
Perdue Chicken *Daisy Martinez*	**84**	
Australian Lamb *Lauren Purcell &* *Anne Purcell Grissinger*	**86**	
Marine Harvest *Anne Willan*	**89**	
SeaMazz *Nick Malgieri*	**92**	
BC Hot House *Jerry Traunfeld*	**95**	
McCormick/Garafalo *Mark Bittman*	**98**	
Cargill Meat Solutions *Stephen Giunta*	**100**	
Alpine Fresh *Giuliano Hazan*	**102**	
Delano Farms *Dave Lieberman*	**104**	

Bill & Cheryl Jamison

Tangy Thai Chicken

Bill and Cheryl Jamison are among the nation's most lauded chefs, with three James Beard awards and numerous other honors to their credit. Called "America's first couple of outdoor cooking," they can be found barbecuing and grilling on NBC's Today Show, the Food Network and QVC. Their next book, The Complete Guide to Outdoor Cooking and Entertaining, is due in late spring 2006. For more about Bill and Cheryl, see their Web site, www.cookingwiththejamisons.com.

Creative Cooking The Costco Way

69

Tangy Thai Chicken
FOSTER FARMS ◀
All recipes developed by Bill and Cheryl Jamison

1 tablespoon Thai red or green curry paste, or more to taste
2 teaspoons peanut oil or vegetable oil
1 14- or 15-ounce can coconut milk
Salt or Asian fish sauce (optional)
4 medium to large Foster Farms* boneless, skinless chicken breasts, pounded 1/2 inch thick
Sweet Thai red chili sauce
Chopped peanuts and/or chopped fresh mint, basil or cilantro, for garnish

1. Combine curry paste and oil in a bowl; stir until the paste is softened. Mix in three-quarters of coconut milk and taste the mixture. If it tastes bland now, it will taste even blander on the chicken, so add more curry paste, and salt if needed, until it is pleasantly pungent. If it's too spicy, add a little more coconut milk.

2. Place chicken in a zippered plastic bag, pour in marinade and seal. Toss to coat chicken evenly. Let sit at room temperature for 20 minutes. For a more intense flavor, marinate for up to several hours, refrigerated.

3. Fire up the grill, bringing the heat to medium.

4. Drain chicken and discard marinade. Grill chicken for 10-12 minutes, turning onto each side twice and rotating to get crisscross grill marks. After chicken has faced the fire once, brush with a few tablespoons of chili sauce. The chicken is ready when it's white throughout but still juicy and the sauce is a bit chewy and caramelized in spots.

5. Serve chicken breasts whole or thickly sliced and mounded on a platter. Sprinkle with chopped peanuts or herbs or both, and accompany with additional chili sauce. Makes 4 servings.

From Good Times, Good Grilling, by Cheryl and Bill Jamison (©2005, HarperCollins Publishers)
*Brands may vary by region; substitute a similar product.

Tex-Mex Wings with Pico de Gallo
FOSTER FARMS ▲

3 pounds Foster Farms* chicken wing drummettes, or 3-3 1/4 pounds other wing sections

MARINADE
1 12-ounce can or bottle of beer
1/4 cup cider vinegar
2 tablespoons chili powder
2 tablespoons packed brown sugar
2 tablespoons molasses
2 tablespoons ketchup or chili sauce
1 tablespoon Dijon mustard
1 teaspoon vegetable oil
1 plump garlic clove, minced
1/2 teaspoon salt

PICO DE GALLO
1 1/2 cups cooked black beans, rinsed and drained
2 plum tomatoes, diced to about the same size as the beans
1 small onion, diced to about the same size as the beans
1 plump garlic clove, minced
1 tablespoon minced fresh cilantro
1 teaspoon cider vinegar
1 teaspoon vegetable oil
Salt

1. Combine the marinade ingredients in a bowl. Place chicken in a zippered plastic bag and pour in the marinade. Seal and toss to coat evenly. Refrigerate for at least several hours, preferably overnight.

2. Shortly before grilling the chicken, prepare the Pico de Gallo: Gently combine all ingredients in a medium bowl. Refrigerate until ready to serve.

3. Empty the marinade into a saucepan. Bring it to a vigorous boil over high heat and continue boiling until reduced by about half; keep warm.

4. Heat the grill to medium. Grill chicken wings for 4-5 minutes, turning to cook all surfaces, then grill and brush with marinade over the next 5 minutes. Let cook for another couple of minutes without glazing so the sauce crisps up a bit. The chicken should be cooked through.

5. Serve warm with Pico de Gallo. Makes 6 servings.

From Chicken on the Grill, by Cheryl and Bill Jamison (©2004, HarperCollins Publishers)
*Brands may vary by region; substitute a similar product.

Chipotle Chicken Salpicón
FOSTER FARMS ▼

Salpicón means "hodgepodge" in Spanish, in this case an edible Mexican hodge-podge of a salad bursting with cubes of tender chicken and vegetables bound together with a mildly spicy dressing. It's a great way to use chicken that's grilled ahead, giving you a chance to mingle and munch with your guests when they arrive

DRESSING
- 1/4 cup plus 2 tablespoons vegetable oil
- 1/4 cup fresh orange or tangerine juice
- 1 tablespoon fresh lime juice
- 1 minced canned chipotle chile and 1 tablespoon adobo sauce from a can of chipotle chiles, *or* 2 tablespoons chipotle ketchup
- 1 garlic clove, minced
- Salt and freshly ground pepper to taste

- 1-1 1/4 pounds Foster Farms* boneless, skinless chicken breasts, pounded 1/2 inch thick
- 1 15-ounce can chick peas, drained and rinsed
- 4 ounces mild cheese, such as Monterey Jack, asadero or mild Cheddar, diced
- 1 cucumber, peeled, seeded and diced
- 1 small tomato, diced
- 1/2 small red onion, finely diced
- 1 ripe avocado, cubed
- Cilantro leaves

1. Whisk together the dressing ingredients. Spoon 3 tablespoons of the dressing over the chicken, turning it once, then cover and let sit at room temperature while you get the grill going.

2. Fire up the grill, bringing the heat to medium.

3. Grill chicken, uncovered, over medium heat for 10-12 minutes, turning onto each side twice and rotating to get crisscross grill marks. The chicken is ready when it's white throughout but still juicy and the dressing is a bit caramelized in spots. If you like a slightly crusty surface, leave chicken on the grill an extra minute or two.

4. When chicken is cool enough to handle, cut into a neat dice, about the size of the chick peas and vegetables. You want to get a bit of everything in most bites.

5. In a large bowl, toss together chicken, chick peas, cheese, cucumber, tomato and onion with most of the dressing. (The salpicón can be made ahead to this point and refrigerated up to overnight.) Add the avocado and, if you wish, more dressing, and combine gently.

6. Spoon onto a platter, scatter with cilantro and serve. Makes 6 servings.

From Good Times, Good Grilling, *by Cheryl and Bill Jamison (©2005, HarperCollins Publishers)*
Brands may vary by region; substitute a similar product.

Susan Lamb Parenti

Susan Lamb Parenti brings more than 20 years' experience in the culinary world to the Swift & Company product development team. She heads Parenti Partners, Ltd., a culinary consulting practice, and served for the National Cattlemen's Beef Association, managing various aspects of the prestigious National Beef Cook-Off and the Beef: It's What's For Dinner ad campaign. Parenti also co-authored the 200-page Skinny Beef *cookbook.*

Mexican Pork Cassoulet with Chipotle Cream
SWIFT ◄

All recipes developed by Susan Lamb Parenti

1 Swift Natural Pork Tenderloin (about 1 1/4 pounds)
1 tablespoon olive oil
Salt and pepper
1 medium onion, chopped
2 garlic cloves, minced
1 15 1/2-ounce can black beans, rinsed and drained
1/2 cup frozen corn
1 15-ounce jar mild salsa
Chopped cilantro and lime wedges, for garnish (optional)

CHIPOTLE CREAM
1/2 cup sour cream
2 teaspoons minced chipotle peppers in adobo sauce

1. Cut pork tenderloin crosswise into 2-inch-wide medallions. Press lightly to flatten.
2. Heat olive oil in a large nonstick skillet over medium heat. Place pork medallions in the skillet and cook for 8-10 minutes, turning once. Remove and season to taste with salt and pepper. Set aside.
3. In the same skillet, cook onion and garlic until tender. Add beans, corn and salsa; bring to a simmer. Return pork to the skillet and cook for 5-7 minutes, or until heated through.
4. Prepare Chipotle Cream: Combine sour cream and chipotle peppers.
5. Serve cassoulet with Chipotle Cream, garnished with cilantro and lime wedges. Makes 4 servings.

Swift & Company®

Mustard-Pepper-Crusted Pork Rack
SWIFT ▲

1/4 cup country-style Dijon mustard
1 1/2 teaspoons dried thyme
1 teaspoon cracked black pepper
1 7-rib Swift Natural Pork Rack (4-5 pounds)

1. Preheat oven to 325°F.
2. Combine mustard, thyme and pepper; spread evenly over pork roast.
3. Place roast in a shallow roasting pan. Insert an ovenproof meat thermometer so the tip is centered in the thickest part, not resting in fat. Do not add water or cover.
4. Roast for 2-2 1/4 hours, or until the thermometer registers 155°F, for medium. Remove from the oven and let stand for 15 minutes (temperature will rise to 160°F). Makes 8-10 servings.

Chef's Choice ∎

Beef Teriyaki Kabobs with Pineapple Sesame Rice
SWIFT ▼

8 9-inch bamboo skewers
2 Swift Premium Teriyaki
   Seasoned Beef Shoulder Filets
   (about 1 1/4 pounds)
2 medium red or green bell
   peppers, cut into 1-inch pieces
1 medium red onion, cut into
   1/2-inch wedges

PINEAPPLE SESAME RICE

2 cups cooked jasmine rice
1 14-ounce can pineapple chunks
   in heavy syrup, drained,
   coarsely chopped,
   juice reserved
1 jalapeño pepper, seeded
   and minced
1/4 cup chopped fresh cilantro
1 tablespoon fresh lime juice
1 teaspoon dark sesame oil
1 tablespoon toasted
   sesame seeds

1. Soak bamboo skewers in water for 10 minutes; drain.

2. Cut beef into 1 1/2-inch pieces. Alternately thread beef, peppers and onion pieces onto skewers.

3. Place kabobs on a grill over medium ash-covered coals. Grill, covered, for 6-8 minutes for medium-rare to medium, turning occasionally and brushing with reserved pineapple juice.

4. Prepare Pineapple Sesame Rice: Combine all ingredients; serve with kabobs. Makes 4 servings.

Tip: For Pork Teriyaki Kabobs, substitute 1 Swift Natural Pork Tenderloin for beef. Place pork pieces in a food-safe plastic bag; add 1/2 cup prepared teriyaki sauce, 1 teaspoon grated fresh ginger and 1 tablespoon dark sesame oil. Close bag and marinate for 30 minutes. Remove pork from marinade; discard marinade. Increase grilling time to about 10-12 minutes for medium doneness.

Leanne Ely

Italian Turkey Meatloaf

Leanne Ely is the author of several books, including the upcoming Saving Dinner for the Holidays. According to Woman's Day Magazine, she is "the expert on family cooking." Her broadcast experience includes QVC, HGTV's Simple Solutions, ABC Family's Living the Life and more. She is the family lifestyle columnist for eDiets.com, whose 13 million readers make it the number one e-zine on the Internet. She offers subscribers weekly menus on her Web site, www.savingdinner.com.

Italian Turkey Meatloaf
TARANTINO ◀
Recipe developed by Leanne Ely

1 large egg
1/2 14 1/2-ounce can diced tomatoes with Italian herbs, undrained
1/2 cup finely chopped onion
1/3 cup minced fresh parsley
1/2 cup oats
1/3 cup grated Parmesan cheese
Salt and pepper
5 Tarantino's* Italian sausage links (or 1 pound), removed
   from casings
1/2 pound ground turkey
1/3 cup prepared spaghetti sauce

1. Preheat oven to 375°F.
2. In a large bowl, beat the egg. Stir in tomatoes, onion, parsley, oats, Parmesan, and salt and pepper to taste.
3. Mix in Italian sausage and ground turkey by hand just until blended.
4. Form into a large meatloaf on a baking sheet (such as a jelly-roll pan), patting to remove any air spaces.
5. Bake for 1 hour. Top with spaghetti sauce and continue baking for 15-30 minutes. Let stand for 10 minutes before serving. Makes 5 servings.

Serving Suggestion: Pasta with a little shaved Romano cheese on top, steamed broccoli and baked butternut squash are good accompaniments.

From Saving Dinner, by Leanne Ely (© 2003, Ballantine Books)
*Brands may vary by region; substitute a similar product.

Italian Sausage Kabobs
TARANTINO ▲

1 pound Tarantino's* mild Italian sausages
1 large red bell pepper, cut into wedges
1 large green bell pepper, cut into wedges
2 fresh tomatoes, cut into wedges
1/2 pound fresh whole medium mushrooms
1 large onion, cut into wedges
1 teaspoon balsamic vinegar
1/4 cup olive oil

1. Preheat barbecue or broiler.
2. Cut each sausage into 3 pieces. Thread on 10-inch skewers, alternating with bell peppers, tomatoes, mushrooms and onion.
3. Mix vinegar and olive oil in a bowl for basting.
4. Barbecue or broil the kabobs on medium heat for 20 minutes, basting and turning occasionally.
5. Serve over rice or polenta. Makes 4 servings.

*Brands may vary by region; substitute a similar product.

Baked Pasta with Sausage and Peppers
TARANTINO ▼

1 1/2 pounds Tarantino's* mild Italian sausages, cut into 1-inch chunks
1 large onion, sliced
1 large green bell pepper, sliced
1 large red bell pepper, sliced
4 garlic cloves, sliced
1 28-ounce can diced tomatoes in puree
1 15-ounce can tomato puree
Salt
1 pound penne pasta
8 ounces shredded mozzarella cheese
1/2 cup freshly grated Romano cheese

1. Preheat oven to 400°F.

2. In a nonstick pan, cook sausage over medium-high heat until browned, stirring occasionally. Drain fat, then reduce heat to medium.

3. Add onion, peppers and garlic; cook for about 10 minutes, or until vegetables are tender. Stir in diced tomatoes, tomato puree and 1/4 teaspoon salt; simmer on low for 10 minutes.

4. Meanwhile, bring a large pot of water to a boil with a dash of salt. Add pasta and cook until almost done. Drain pasta, return it to the pot, and stir in the sauce and mozzarella.

5. Transfer pasta mixture to a 9-by-13-inch baking dish and sprinkle with Romano cheese. Bake, uncovered, for 20 minutes, or until browned.

6. Let stand for 10 minutes before serving. Makes 8-10 servings.

*Brands may vary by region; substitute a similar product.

Mario Batali

Mario Batali shares his passion for the authentic spirit of Italian food through his restaurants, food and wine shops, cookbooks, television shows and products. His latest cookbook is Molto Italiano, *published by HarperCollins. Mario's mantra is, "Al tavolo non s'invecchia mai—at the table, one never gets old."*

Chicken Thighs with Saffron, Green Olives and Mint
GOLD KIST FARMS ◄

All recipes developed by Mario Batali

12 Gold Kist Farms* boneless, skinless chicken thighs
 (2 1/2-3 pounds)
Salt and pepper
All-purpose flour
1/4 cup extra-virgin olive oil
2 large red onions, thinly sliced
1/2 teaspoon saffron threads
1 cup small green olives
1 medium carrot, finely chopped
3 cups chicken stock
6 servings of couscous
1/2 cup fresh mint leaves

1. Season chicken thighs liberally with salt and pepper; dredge in flour. In a heavy-bottomed casserole, heat olive oil over medium-high heat until smoking. Add 6 thighs at a time and brown well on all sides. Transfer to a plate and repeat with the remaining thighs.
2. Add onions and saffron to the casserole. Cook over low heat until onions have softened, 8-10 minutes. Add olives, carrot and chicken stock and bring to a boil.
3. Return chicken to the casserole, submerging in the stock, and bring to a boil. Lower heat, cover the pot tightly and simmer for 1 hour. Remove the lid and cook for 10 minutes.
4. Place couscous on a serving platter. Arrange chicken thighs on the couscous. Season the sauce with salt and pepper to taste and stir in mint leaves. Pour the sauce over the chicken thighs and serve. Makes 6 servings.
Brands may vary by region; substitute a similar product.

Chicken Hunter's Style
GOLD KIST FARMS ▲

2 garlic cloves, minced
1 branch rosemary,
 leaves only, minced
Salt
Freshly ground black pepper
1/2 cup extra-virgin olive oil
8 Gold Kist Farms* chicken
 drumsticks, rinsed and
 patted dry
2 large yellow onions,
 coarsely chopped
1 pound portobello mushrooms,
 stems removed, cut into
 1-inch cubes
4 ounces pancetta, cut into
 1/8-inch dice
4 ribs celery, cut into 1-inch pieces
2 cups basic tomato sauce
1 cup dry white wine
1 cup chicken stock
Pinch of sugar
Pinch of red pepper flakes

1. In a large bowl, combine garlic, rosemary, and salt and pepper to taste. Add enough olive oil (3-4 tablespoons) to make a somewhat dry paste. Add chicken and rub the paste evenly over the pieces of chicken. Cover and refrigerate for 2 hours.
2. In a Dutch oven, heat the remaining 1/4 cup olive oil over high heat until smoking. Brush off the excess rub and sear the chicken, in batches if necessary, until browned on all sides. Transfer to a plate lined with paper towels.
3. Add onions, mushrooms, pancetta and celery to the pot and cook until onions are golden brown and pancetta has rendered its fat, about 8 minutes.
4. Drain off excess oil, then add tomato sauce and wine, stirring with a wooden spoon to dislodge the browned bits from the bottom of the pot. Add stock, sugar and red pepper and bring to a boil.
5. Return chicken to the pot, cover and cook for 20 minutes. Uncover and cook for 15-20 minutes, or until cooked through. Transfer chicken to a festive platter, top with the sauce and serve. Makes 4 servings.
Brands may vary by region; substitute a similar product.

Agnolotti
GOLD KIST FARMS ▼

8 tablespoons (1 stick) unsalted butter, divided

1 medium Spanish onion, cut into 1/8-inch dice

1 Gold Kist Farms* boneless, skinless chicken breast (about 6 ounces), cut into 2-inch pieces

4 ounces sweet Italian sausage, removed from casings and cut into 2-inch lengths

1/4 cup ricotta

1/4 cup grated Italian fontina

2 tablespoons fresh marjoram leaves

3 tablespoons fresh goat cheese

1/4 cup finely chopped Italian parsley, plus 1 tablespoon cut in thin strips

1/4 teaspoon freshly grated nutmeg

Salt

Freshly ground black pepper

1 1/4 pounds prepared pasta dough

4 ounces porcini or cremini mushrooms, sliced paper-thin

1/4 cup freshly grated Parmigiano-Reggiano cheese

1. To make the filling, heat 4 tablespoons butter over medium heat in a 10- to 12-inch sauté pan until it foams and subsides. Add onion and cook until soft and golden brown, 7-8 minutes.

2. Add chicken and sausage and cook until cooked through, about 10 minutes. Remove from the heat and let cool.

3. Transfer chicken mixture to a food processor and pulse until finely chopped. Transfer to a medium bowl, add ricotta, fontina, marjoram, goat cheese, chopped parsley, nutmeg, and salt and pepper to taste, and mix well. Set aside.

4. To make the agnolotti, divide pasta dough into 4 pieces. Roll out each one through the thinnest setting on a pasta machine and lay on a lightly floured work surface. Cut each sheet lengthwise in half to form strips 2 inches wide and 24 inches long.

5. Starting 1 inch from one end, place 1 tablespoon of filling every 2 inches along the bottom of each strip. Fold the top half of the pasta over the bottom and press the edges together to seal, gently pressing out any air pockets.

6. Using a fluted round pastry cutter, cut out the agnolotti. Transfer to a baking sheet dusted with flour.

7. Bring 6 quarts of water to a boil in a large pot and add 2 tablespoons salt. Drop the agnolotti carefully into the boiling water, lower the heat and cook at a brisk simmer until tender, 3-4 minutes.

8. Meanwhile, melt remaining butter in a 10- to 12-inch sauté pan over medium heat. Add mushrooms, season to taste with salt and pepper, and sauté until tender.

9. Drain the agnolotti, add to the mushrooms and sprinkle with remaining parsley and Parmigiano-Reggiano. Toss for about 1 minute to coat with sauce. Transfer to a plate and serve. Makes 6 servings.

Brands may vary by region; substitute a similar product.

Michael Brando

Chef Michael Brando studied culinary arts internationally and has achieved Master Chef status. Brando is now celebrating his 36th professional year in culinary arts and is a gold and silver medal winner in several international culinary competitions. During the past 10 years, Brando has focused his culinary career in the area of product development for both the food-service and retail marketplace. Throughout that period, he has successfully developed and launched several hundred innovative products.

Bacon-Wrapped Marinated Pork Loin
FARMLAND ▲
All recipes developed by Michael Brando

¹/₄ cup soy sauce

¹/₄ cup packed light brown sugar

2 tablespoons dry sherry

1¹/₂ teaspoons dried minced onions

1 teaspoon ground cinnamon

2 tablespoons olive oil

1 pinch garlic powder

1¹/₂ pounds Farmland Boneless Pork Loin

8-10 slices Farmland* Hickory Smoked Bacon

Wooden skewers or toothpicks

1. Combine soy sauce, brown sugar, sherry, dried onions, cinnamon, olive oil and garlic powder in a large resealable plastic bag. Seal and mix together. Add pork, seal and marinate in the refrigerator for 6-12 hours.

2. Partially cook bacon, rendering some of the fat, and drain. Wrap bacon around pork and pin with water-soaked skewers or toothpicks to hold bacon in place.

3. Preheat grill to medium-high to high heat.

4. Grill meat over hot coals until well done, approximately 15-25 minutes. Cut into medallions and serve. Makes 4-6 servings.

Brands may vary by region; substitute a similar product.

Applewood-Smoked Bacon and Kielbasa with Baked Beans "Angus" Style
CARANDO/FARMER'S ▲

12 ounces Farmer's* Applewood Smoked Thick Bacon, finely diced

1 cup diced yellow onion

3 garlic cloves, finely chopped

2 small jalapeño peppers, seeded and finely chopped

12 ounces Carando* Kielbasa, sliced 1/4 inch thick

3/4 cup ketchup

1/2 cup prepared yellow mustard

1/2 teaspoon ground ginger

1 teaspoon dry yellow mustard

1/2 cup dark rum

3 tablespoons light brown sugar

2 tablespoons honey

1/4 cup molasses

1/4 cup light corn syrup

1/2 tablespoon hot pepper sauce

2 tablespoons Worcestershire sauce

1 15- to 19-ounce can *each* garbanzo beans (chick peas), black beans and great northern beans

1. In a large saucepan or pot, cook bacon over medium heat for about 12 minutes, stirring continually with a wooden spoon, until browned and crispy.

2. Add onion, garlic and jalapeños. Lower the heat and cook for 7 minutes, or until the onion is translucent.

3. Add all remaining ingredients except beans. Increase the heat and bring to a boil, then reduce heat and simmer, stirring mixture often, for 15 minutes.

4. Drain all the beans, rinse gently under cold running water and then drain again. Add to the mixture and stir well to combine. Simmer gently, uncovered, for approximately 1 hour. Makes 6 hearty servings.

Brands may vary by region; substitute a similar product.

Hawaiian Wraps with Spiral-Cut Ham
KIRKLAND SIGNATURE/CARANDO ▲

4 spinach tortillas

4 tablespoons pineapple cream cheese spread

4 teaspoons honey mustard

8 slices Kirkland Signature Spiral-Cut Ham by Carando*

4 slices Colby-Monterey Jack cheese

1 medium tomato, thinly sliced

1/2 cup shredded lettuce

1. Place tortillas on a microwave-safe plate and microwave on high for 30 seconds.

2. Place a tortilla on a flat surface and spread with 1 tablespoon cream cheese up to 1 inch from the edges. Top with 1 teaspoon honey mustard.

3. Place 2 ham slices on honey mustard. Add 1 cheese slice.

4. Top with 1 tomato slice and 2 tablespoons lettuce.

5. Fold up one edge of tortilla about 1 inch and then roll in the shape of a cylinder. Repeat with remaining tortillas. Makes 4 servings.

Brands may vary by region; substitute a similar product.

Nacho Ribs
CURLEY'S ▲

1 16-ounce can refried beans

8 ounces tortilla chips, any flavor

40 ounces Curly's* Fully Cooked Hickory Smoked Baby Back Pork Ribs

3 ounces shredded cheese (Colby/Jack, taco)

4 ounces prepared salsa

2 ounces sour cream

1/2 tomato, diced

1 jalapeño pepper, diced

2 green onions, chopped

1. Preheat oven to 350°F.

2. Place refried beans in the center of a large ovenproof dish.

3. Crush tortilla chips and place on a plate.

4. Slice pork into individual riblets and coat with crushed tortilla chips.
Arrange coated ribs around refried beans. Bake for 20-22 minutes, or until
heated through.

5. Remove from the oven, sprinkle with cheese and ladle salsa over the beans.
Garnish with sour cream, tomato, jalapeño and green onions. Makes 4 servings.

Brands may vary by region; substitute a similar product.

Pork Tenderloin with Cilantro Lime Pesto and Smoky Bacon Bits
SMITHFIELD ▲

1 tablespoon minced garlic

2 tablespoons minced fresh ginger

1/4 cup minced green onions

1 tablespoon minced fresh cilantro

1 teaspoon minced jalapeño pepper

1/2 teaspoon freshly ground pepper

2 tablespoons lime juice

2 tablespoons orange juice

2 tablespoons olive oil

11/2-2 pounds Smithfield Pork Tenderloin

1/2 cup grated jalapeño jack cheese

1/4 cup sunflower or pumpkin seeds, toasted and chopped

1/2 cup Smithfield* Real Crumbled Bacon

1. To prepare the pesto, combine the first 8 ingredients in a food processor
or blender and puree. Slowly add olive oil until the mixture thickens.

2. Cut tenderloin in half lengthwise and lay out flat. Spread half of pesto over
tenderloin and sprinkle with grated cheese and seeds. Sprinkle with bacon.

3. Close tenderloin and tie with kitchen string to secure. Spread remaining
pesto over tenderloin and refrigerate for several hours or overnight.

4. Preheat oven to 400°F.

5. Place tenderloin on a rack and bake until firm, 25-30 minutes (internal
temperature of 155°F). Remove from the oven, cover and let rest for 10 minutes.

6. Slice pork and serve with reserved juices. Makes 4 servings.

Brands may vary by region; substitute a similar product.

Daisy Martinez

Daisy Martinez, star of her own public television cooking show, Daisy Cooks!, attended the French Culinary Institute and runs her own catering business, The Passionate Palate. Her first cookbook, DAISY COOKS! Latin Flavors That Will Rock Your World, a tie-in to her cooking show, was published this year by Hyperion Books.

Cracker Jack Chicken
PERDUE CHICKEN ◄

6 pieces Kirkland Signature/Perdue* Individually Frozen Boneless, Skinless Chicken Breasts (about 3 pounds), thawed in the refrigerator overnight
Fine sea or kosher salt
Freshly ground black pepper
6 thin slices serrano ham, prosciutto or deli ham
6 pinkie-size pieces Monterey Jack or Havarti cheese
1/4 cup all-purpose flour

Canola oil
3 large eggs
1 cup Italian-style bread crumbs

BÉCHAMEL SAUCE
4 tablespoons butter
1/4 cup all-purpose flour
2 cups milk, hot
3 sprigs fresh thyme
1 bay leaf
Fine sea or kosher salt
Tiny pinch of nutmeg

1. Starting from the thick side, slice chicken breasts almost in half horizontally. Open up and pound with a mallet to just under 1/2 inch thick.
2. Season breasts with salt and pepper. Lay 1 ham slice on each, leaving a 1/2-inch border. Place cheese along edge. Fold chicken over cheese and roll into a compact bundle. Tie with kitchen twine at 1-inch intervals. Roll bundles in flour to coat, tapping off excess.
3. Heat 1/4 inch oil in a large heavy skillet over medium-low. Add as many chicken rolls as will fit without touching. Cook, turning often, until golden brown and cooked through, about 10 minutes or until internal temperature reaches 170°F. Remove and let cool. Remove twine from chicken.
4. Meanwhile, make the Béchamel Sauce: Melt butter in a small saucepan over medium-low heat. Stir in flour and cook, whisking, for 4 minutes. Slowly whisk in milk. Add thyme and bay leaf. Bring to a boil, whisking constantly. Lower heat and simmer, whisking occasionally, until thickened and smooth, about 15 minutes. Stir in salt to taste and nutmeg.
5. Line a baking sheet with waxed paper. Dip chicken rolls in Béchamel to coat and set on the waxed paper. Refrigerate until sauce is set, at least 45 minutes.
6. Beat eggs in a shallow bowl until foamy. Spread bread crumbs in another shallow bowl. Dip chicken in eggs to coat. Roll in bread crumbs until coated, then set on a baking sheet.
7. Heat 4 inches of oil in a large heavy pot over medium heat to about 390°F. Slip 3 chicken rolls into oil and cook until golden brown, about 2 1/2 minutes. Remove to paper towels. Repeat with remaining chicken. Makes 6 servings.

* Brands may vary by region; substitute a similar product.

Crispy Chicken Bits
PERDUE CHICKEN ▲
All recipes developed by Daisy Martinez

1 1/2 pounds Perdue* Individually Frozen Chicken Tenderloins, thawed in the refrigerator overnight
1 teaspoon dry adobo seasoning
1 1/2 tablespoons cider vinegar (or your favorite)
Vegetable or canola oil
All-purpose flour

1. Cut chicken into pinkie-size strips. Place in a bowl and toss with adobo seasoning and vinegar until coated. Marinate, covered, at room temperature for up to 30 minutes or in the refrigerator up to 24 hours. Drain the chicken thoroughly.
2. Pour 3 inches of vegetable oil into a deep heavy pot. Heat over medium-high heat until the tip of a wooden spoon handle gives off a very lively sizzle when dipped into the oil (about 390°F).
3. While the oil is heating, dredge the chicken in flour until coated. Tap off any excess flour.
4. When the oil is hot, carefully slip as many of the floured chicken pieces into the oil as will fit comfortably. Let them bob around, turning them with a spoon once or twice, until deep golden brown and cooked through, about 4 minutes. Remove and drain on paper towels. Repeat with the remaining chicken. Serve hot. Makes 6 snack-size servings.

* Brands may vary by region; substitute a similar product.

French Rack of Lamb with
Rosemary Mustard Cream

Lauren Purcell & Anne Purcell Grissinger

*New York City-based sister team Lauren Purcell and Anne
Purcell Grissinger are the authors of* Cocktail Parties, Straight
Up! Easy Hors D'oeuvres, Delicious Drinks, and Inspired
Ideas for Entertaining with Style, *published by John Wiley &
Sons. The Purcell sisters grew up in the small-town South and
perfected their entertaining expertise over 15 years of throwing
parties in Manhattan, marrying Southern hospitality with city
chic. More of their recipes and down-to-earth advice can be
found at* www.purcellsisters.com.

THE
AUSTRALIAN LAMB
COMPANY INC.

French Rack of Lamb with Rosemary Mustard Cream
AUSTRALIAN LAMB ◀

Recipe developed by Lauren Purcell & Anne Purcell Grissinger

2 teaspoons minced garlic

2 teaspoons finely chopped rosemary

$^1/_2$ teaspoon salt

$^1/_2$ teaspoon freshly ground black pepper

$^1/_2$ teaspoon dry mustard

2 teaspoons olive oil

3 French racks of Australian lamb (8 ribs per rack)

ROSEMARY MUSTARD CREAM

$^1/_2$ cup dry white wine

$^1/_4$ cup chopped shallots

1 cup whipping cream

2 tablespoons Dijon mustard

2 teaspoons finely chopped rosemary

Salt and pepper

1. Prepare Rosemary Mustard Cream: In a small saucepan, boil wine and shallots over high heat until liquid is reduced to about $^1/_3$ cup, about 5 minutes. Reduce the heat to medium and add cream. Simmer until the sauce is slightly thickened and reduced to just under 1 cup, about 30 minutes. Add mustard and rosemary and simmer for 2 minutes. Add salt and pepper to taste. Set aside (the cream will continue to thicken slightly as it cools).

2. Preheat oven to 500°F.

3. In a small bowl, combine garlic, rosemary, salt, pepper and dry mustard. Add olive oil and stir to make a paste. Coat the top and underside of the lamb racks with the paste.

4. Heat a cast iron or other non-nonstick pan over high heat. When very hot, place a lamb rack in the pan, meat side down, and sear for 1-2 minutes to brown. (You may have to press the ends of the rack down with a spatula so they meet the pan's surface.) Flip to sear the underside. Repeat with each rack, then transfer to a roasting pan.

5. Roast for 20-25 minutes for medium-rare, 25-30 minutes for medium. Remove from the oven and let sit for 10 minutes.

6. Slice racks between ribs and serve each guest 4 chops with Rosemary Mustard Cream alongside. Makes 6 servings.

Orange-and-Apricot Leg of Lamb with Almond Couscous
AUSTRALIAN LAMB ▲

1 boneless Australian leg of lamb

Grated peel and juice of 2 large oranges

8 dried apricots, plumped in hot water, finely diced

1 teaspoon ground cardamom

2 teaspoons ground cumin

1 teaspoon ground cinnamon

2 tablespoons honey, warmed

ALMOND COUSCOUS

3 cups chicken stock

2 cups pearl (Israeli) couscous

$^1/_2$ cup chopped fresh cilantro or parsley

3 green onions, sliced

Grated peel and juice of 1 lemon

2 tablespoons olive oil

Salt and freshly ground pepper

$^1/_2$ cup sliced or slivered almonds, toasted

1. Trim lamb and cut shallow slashes half an inch apart over the top.

2. In a small bowl, combine grated orange peel, apricots, cardamom, cumin, cinnamon and honey; mix well. Massage all over the lamb and into the slashes. Cover and let stand at room temperature for 20-30 minutes.

3. Preheat oven to 375°F.

4. Place lamb on a rack in a baking dish and roast for 1 $^1/_2$-2 hours, or until internal temperature is 130-135°F for medium-rare, or until cooked as desired. Remove from the oven, cover loosely with foil and let rest for 10-15 minutes before carving.

5. Meanwhile, prepare Almond Couscous: Place chicken stock and reserved orange juice in a saucepan and bring to a boil. Stir in couscous, cover, remove from the heat and let stand for 10 minutes, or until all liquid is absorbed and the couscous is tender.

6. Transfer couscous to a bowl and fluff with a fork. Toss with cilantro, green onions, lemon juice and grated peel, and olive oil. Season to taste with salt and pepper. Just before serving, sprinkle with almonds.

7. Carve the lamb and serve with couscous and a spinach salad, if desired. Makes 8 servings.

Tandoori Lamb with Cumin Sauce
AUSTRALIAN LAMB ▼

Recipe developed by Lauren Purcell &
Anne Purcell Grissinger

2 pounds boneless leg of lamb, trimmed of fat and cut into 1-inch cubes (you will have about 60 pieces)

MARINADE
2 cups plain yogurt
2 tablespoons ground coriander
2 tablespoons paprika
2 tablespoons fresh lemon juice
1 ½ tablespoons ground cumin
1 ½ tablespoons ground ginger
½ teaspoon turmeric
½ teaspoon ground cardamom
½ teaspoon salt
1 garlic clove, minced

CUMIN SAUCE
¾ cup sour cream
¾ cup plain yogurt
1 tablespoon fresh lemon juice
1 teaspoon ground cumin
salt and pepper to taste

1. Combine all marinade ingredients in a bowl and mix thoroughly. Add lamb, stirring to fully coat each cube. Cover and refrigerate overnight.
2. Prepare Cumin Sauce: Mix all ingredients together in a bowl. (This can be made 2 days ahead and refrigerated, covered.)
3. Preheat the broiler.
4. Remove lamb from the marinade and gently pat off extra marinade with paper towels. Transfer to a lightly oiled broiler pan and broil for 3 minutes. Turn the cubes over and broil for another 2 minutes. The lamb should be slightly pink in the center. Transfer lamb to a plate or cutting board and sprinkle with salt.
5. To serve as a main course: Thread 4-5 pieces of lamb onto a skewer and serve each guest 2 skewers with Cumin Sauce on the side. To serve as appetizers: Place sauce in a bowl in the center of a platter. Arrange lamb around it and provide toothpicks. Makes 6 main-course or 20 appetizer servings.

Spaghetti with Tomatoes, Toasted Garlic and Loads of Herbs
BC HOT HOUSE ▼

1 16-ounce box spaghetti
1/4 cup extra-virgin olive oil
6 garlic cloves, very thinly sliced
6 medium-sized BC Hot House* tomatoes, diced
1 teaspoon kosher salt
2 tablespoons coarsely chopped fresh marjoram or oregano
2 tablespoons coarsely chopped fresh mint
1/2 cup coarsely chopped fresh basil
1/2 cup coarsely chopped fresh Italian parsley
1/2 cup grated Parmigiano-Reggiano cheese

1. Bring a large pot of salted water to a boil. Add spaghetti and cook until tender but still firm.

2. Meanwhile, pour oil into a large skillet set over medium heat. Add garlic and stir until lightly browned and toasted, about 3 minutes.

3. Immediately add tomatoes and salt and toss in the oil until warmed through but not cooked. Remove the skillet from the heat.

4. When the spaghetti is done, drain it and toss with the tomatoes in the skillet (or in the pasta pot if the skillet is not large enough). Sprinkle with the herbs and cheese and toss again.

5. Tip the pasta out onto a large warm platter and serve right away.
Makes 4 servings.

*Brands may vary by region; substitute a similar product.

Mark Bittman

Best-selling cookbook author Mark Bittman is the creator and author of the popular New York Times *weekly column "The Minimalist" and one of the country's best-known and most widely admired food writers. His latest cookbook is* How to Cook Everything: Bittman Takes on America's Chefs, *published in 2005 by John Wiley & Sons, Inc. Bittman is a regular guest on the* Today *show and NPR's* All Things Considered. *For more, see his Web site,* www.howtocookeverything.com.

Penne all'Arrabbiata
McCORMICK/GAROFALO ◄

3 medium garlic cloves, divided
3 tablespoons olive oil, divided
2 tablespoons tomato paste
1 28-ounce can whole tomatoes in juice, chopped
1 McCormick* bay leaf
1 tablespoon chopped McCormick* Gourmet Collection Organic parsley flakes, plus more for garnish
1 tablespoon chopped McCormick* Gourmet Collection Organic basil leaves, plus more for garnish
$^1/_2$ teaspoon McCormick* crushed red pepper
$^1/_4$ cup white wine
1 teaspoon salt
1 pound Garofalo* penne rigate pasta, cooked according to package directions
Freshly grated Parmesan cheese (optional)

1. Chop 1 garlic clove. Heat 1 tablespoon oil in a 3-quart saucepan over medium heat. Add chopped garlic and cook for 30 seconds.
2. Add tomato paste and cook, stirring, for 2 minutes. Add tomatoes in juice and bay leaf; simmer, uncovered, for 30 minutes.
3. Meanwhile, thinly slice remaining 2 garlic cloves. Heat 1 tablespoon oil in a 12-inch skillet over medium heat. Add garlic and cook for 30 seconds, until just beginning to turn pale golden.
4. Add 1 tablespoon parsley, 1 tablespoon basil and crushed red pepper; cook for 30 seconds. Add wine and boil for 30 seconds. Stir into the tomato mixture; add salt and simmer for 4-5 minutes.
5. Toss sauce with hot pasta in a large serving bowl. Drizzle with remaining 1 tablespoon oil. Serve with Parmesan and garnish with parsley and basil, if desired. Makes 4 servings.

Brands may vary by region; substitute a similar product.

Fast and Easy Shrimp Paella
McCORMICK/GAROFALO ▲
Recipe developed by Mark Bittman

4 cups chicken stock
3 tablespoons olive oil
1 medium onion, minced
About 1 teaspoon McCormick* Gourmet Collection paprika
1 teaspoon McCormick* ground cumin
2 cups Spanish (or other) short-grain rice
2 cups raw peeled shrimp, cut into $^1/_2$-inch chunks
Salt
McCormick* Gourmet Collection Organic parsley flakes, for garnish

1. Preheat oven to 450°F. Warm stock in a saucepan.
2. Place an ovenproof 10- or 12-inch skillet over medium-high heat and add oil. A minute later, add onion and cook, stirring occasionally, until translucent and soft, about 5 minutes. Add paprika and cumin and cook 1 minute more.
3. Add rice and cook, stirring occasionally, until glossy, just 1-2 minutes. Stir in shrimp, season liberally with salt and add the warm stock, taking care to avoid the rising steam. Transfer the skillet to the oven.
4. Bake for about 15 minutes, until all the liquid is absorbed and the rice is dry on top. Taste for salt, then garnish with parsley and serve immediately. Makes 4 servings.

Brands may vary by region; substitute a similar product.

Stephen Giunta

Chef Stephen Giunta, a graduate of the Culinary Institute of America and Certified Master Chef, served as personal chef to former President and Mrs. Ronald Reagan. His extensive experience includes serving as associate professor in culinary arts at the Culinary Institute and as corporate chef for Kerry Ingredients in Beloit, Wisconsin. Giunta was a member of the Gold Medal U.S. Culinary Olympic teams in 1984 and 1988.

Sicilian-Style Pot Roast
CARGILL MEAT SOLUTIONS ◄
All recipes developed by Stephen Giunta

1/4 cup extra-virgin olive oil
1 Morton's of Omaha* Beef Pot Roast (2-3 pounds)
1 teaspoon red pepper flakes
3 garlic cloves, chopped
1 cup red wine
1 quart prepared tomato sauce
Grated peel and juice of 1 lemon
1/2 cup kalamata olives, pitted and halved
2 tablespoons chopped fresh Italian parsley

1. Preheat oven to 325°F.
2. In a heavy sauté pan, heat olive oil over medium heat. Add red pepper flakes and garlic to the sauté pan; cook until the aroma is apparent. Add wine and simmer until the liquid is reduced by half. Add tomato sauce, grated lemon peel and olives; bring to a simmer.
3. Place the pot roast in the sauce, cover the pan and gently heat until an internal temperature of 150°F is reached (approximately 30 minutes).
4. Add lemon juice and chopped parsley to the sauce and check for seasoning.
5. Serve with polenta, broccoli and crusty bread. Makes 4 servings.

* Brands may vary by region; substitute a similar product.

French Dip
CARGILL MEAT SOLUTIONS ▲

GARLIC BUTTER
1 stick unsalted butter, softened
1 teaspoon chopped fresh garlic
2-3 drops lemon juice
Salt and pepper to taste

4 ciabatta rolls, halved (French bread works as well)
16 ounces thinly sliced Emmber Classic* roast beef, warm
8 ounces prepared au jus, hot

1. To make garlic butter, combine all ingredients and mix well.
2. To build the sandwiches, spread 1 tablespoon garlic butter on each side of ciabatta rolls. Toast under a medium broiler or in a toaster oven until golden brown and crisp, about 4-5 minutes.
3. Place 4 ounces warm roast beef in each roll.
4. Serve with individual ramekins of hot au jus on the side.
Makes 4 servings.

* Brands may vary by region; substitute a similar product.

Giuliano Hazan

Giuliano Hazan is the author of How to Cook Italian *and two previous cookbooks,* The Classic Pasta Cookbook, *nominated for a James Beard Award in 1994, and* Every Night Italian. *Hazan teaches cooking at schools throughout North America and abroad, including Italy, where along with his partner, Marilisa Allegrini, he and his wife, Lael, have a school in Verona's wine country.*

Blueberry and Mango Fruit Salad
ALPINE FRESH ◀

All recipes developed by Giuliano Hazan

3 Alpine Fresh* ripe mangoes
2 pints Alpine Fresh* blueberries
6 tablespoons sugar
1 lemon
1/2 cup fresh orange juice
2 tablespoons grappa

1. Peel mangoes, slice into bite-size pieces and place in a large serving bowl.
2. Rinse blueberries in cold water, drain and add to the bowl. Add sugar.
3. Grate the zest from the lemon and juice half the lemon. Add zest and juice to the bowl.
4. Add orange juice and grappa. Stir gently, being careful not to damage the berries.
5. Cover the bowl and refrigerate for at least 2 hours and up to 24 hours. Stir once again and serve chilled. Makes 6 servings.

* Brands may vary by region; substitute a similar product.

Risotto with Asparagus and Tomatoes
ALPINE FRESH ▲

3 cups water
1 pound Alpine Fresh* asparagus
Salt
4 cups homemade meat broth or 1/2 each beef and chicken bouillon cube dissolved in 4 cups water
1/2 small yellow onion, finely chopped
3 tablespoons butter, divided
Freshly ground black pepper
8 ounces Alpine Fresh* grape tomatoes
1 3/4 cups rice for risotto
1/4 cup freshly grated Parmigiano-Reggiano cheese

1. Put water in a deep skillet, place over high heat and bring to a boil.
2. Cut off the white woody bottom part of the asparagus spears, then peel the remaining bottom third. Add 1 teaspoon salt to the boiling water, then slide in the asparagus. Cook until tender, 5-6 minutes; remove the asparagus, saving the water. Keep the asparagus water over low heat.
3. Put broth in a pot and bring to a boil. Lower the heat to a simmer.
4. Sauté onion in a heavy-bottomed braising pan with 2 tablespoons butter over medium-high heat until it turns a rich golden color.
5. Cut asparagus into 1-inch lengths. Add to the onion, season to taste with salt and pepper (go easy with the salt) and sauté for 3-4 minutes.
6. Cut tomatoes in half. When asparagus is done, add tomatoes and cook until they begin to soften, 3-4 minutes. Add rice and stir to coat. Add 1 cup of hot asparagus water and continue stirring. When absorbed, continue adding asparagus water until it's all used.
7. Begin adding the broth. Use only enough to produce the consistency of a thick soup, and wait until all the liquid is absorbed before adding more. Continue until the rice is al dente, 20-25 minutes.
8. Remove the risotto from the heat and stir in remaining butter and the Parmigiano-Reggiano. Serve at once. Makes 4 servings.

* Brands may vary by region; substitute a similar product.

Dave Lieberman

Dave Lieberman is the host of his own Food Network show, Good Deal with Dave Lieberman, *and works as a personal chef in and around New York City. His first cookbook,* Young & Hungry: More Than 100 Recipes for Cooking Fresh and Affordable Food for Everyone, *was published by Hyperion Books in April 2005. Lieberman started his first cooking show while a student at Yale. He has settled in New York City but is often seen visiting his hometown of Philadelphia.*

Red Grape, Grape Tomato and Avocado Salad
DELANO FARMS ◀

All recipes developed by Dave Lieberman

1 small ripe Hass avocado
About 25 Delano Farms red grapes, quartered
20 grape tomatoes, halved
1 small yellow bell pepper, cut into 1/8-inch dice
1 small shallot, sliced as thinly as possible
Salt
Freshly ground black pepper
About 15 fresh basil leaves, finely chopped or slivered
Extra-virgin olive oil
Red wine vinegar

1. Cut avocado in half lengthwise and twist to separate the halves. Remove the pit by smacking your chef's knife into the pit and twisting it out.
2. Carefully remove the avocado flesh with a large spoon and slice the avocado halves lengthwise into 1/4-inch slices.
3. Arrange avocado slices on 4 plates. Scatter grapes, tomatoes, bell pepper and shallot around and a little bit on top of the avocado slices.
4. Sprinkle with a couple of pinches of salt and a few grinds of pepper. Scatter basil on top.
5. Finish by drizzling with olive oil and vinegar. Makes 4 servings.

Red Grape White Wine Granita
DELANO FARMS ▲

1 pound Delano Farms seedless red grapes
3/4 cup dry white wine
1/4 cup superfine sugar

1. Place all ingredients in a blender and blend until smooth.
2. Pour into a 2-quart rectangular dish. Freeze until solid, about 3-4 hours.
3. When ready to serve, use a fork to scrape out portions into glasses.
Makes 12-15 servings.

Entrées

Chile-Crusted Sea Scallops with Mango Citrus Salad
ATLANTIC CAPES ◀

SALAD

¹/₄ cup fresh lime juice
¹/₄ cup fresh lemon juice
¹/₄ cup fresh orange juice
2 tablespoons chopped fresh basil
2 tablespoons minced shallot
1 ¹/₄ cups olive oil
Salt and pepper
6 cups mixed salad greens
    (spring mix or assorted greens)
1 ripe mango, peeled and diced
1 red bell pepper, cut into strips
¹/₄ cup chopped fresh cilantro
    or parsley

SCALLOPS

2 tablespoons ground cumin
¹/₄ cup ancho chile powder
¹/₂ tablespoon crushed
    coriander seed
1 teaspoon salt
1 teaspoon ground black pepper
2 pounds Atlantic Capes
    sea scallops
¹/₄ cup olive oil

1. To prepare the salad, combine fruit juices, basil and shallot in a blender; blend until smooth. With the motor running, slowly add olive oil until the mixture is emulsified. Season to taste with salt and pepper.

2. Combine salad greens, mango and half of the bell pepper in a large bowl. Drizzle with a few tablespoons of vinaigrette and toss to coat. Place the salad on a large plate.

3. To prepare the scallops, combine cumin, chile powder, coriander, salt and pepper in a shallow bowl. Dredge one side of each scallop in the spice mixture. Heat olive oil in a large sauté pan until very hot. Cook scallops in the oil, starting with the chile-coated side, for 1-2 minutes on each side.

4. Arrange scallops around the salad mixture. Drizzle everything with a little more vinaigrette. Top with remaining bell pepper slices and cilantro or parsley. Makes 4 servings.

Striped Scallops with Baby Greens
AMERICAN PRIDE SEAFOODS ▲

3 cups balsamic vinegar
¹/₂ cup heavy cream
5 ounces soft goat cheese
2 pounds American Pride U/10 frozen sea scallops, thawed
Salt and pepper
Butter
16 ounces baby salad greens (field, spring or mesclun)
Olive oil
1 cup finely diced red bell pepper
³/₄ cup minced shallots

1. In a saucepan, cook balsamic vinegar over medium-low heat until reduced by half, to a thin syrupy consistency. Once cooled, transfer to a squeeze bottle and refrigerate.

2. In a bowl, thoroughly combine cream and goat cheese. Transfer to a squeeze bottle and refrigerate.

3. Pat scallops dry; season to taste with salt and pepper.

4. Melt butter in a sauté pan over high heat. Before the butter browns, add scallops to the pan. Sear for 2 minutes per side, until opaque and slightly firm, then remove from the pan.

5. Toss greens with a little olive oil, salt and pepper. Divide greens among 5 plates; top each serving with 3-5 scallops, bell pepper and shallots. Drizzle with some of the balsamic reduction, then the goat cheese. Makes 5 servings.

King Crab with Chardonnay Beurre Blanc Sauce
AQUA STAR

2 pounds Aqua Star king crab legs, thawed and prepared according to package directions

BEURRE BLANC SAUCE
1 tablespoon salted butter, plus 1/2 cup (1 stick) cold salted butter, cut into 1/2-inch cubes
2 garlic cloves, minced (or shallots)
1/3 cup Chardonnay
1 tablespoon chopped fresh parsley
Freshly ground white pepper

1. Prepare Beurre Blanc Sauce: In a saucepan, heat 1 tablespoon butter over medium heat. Add garlic or shallots and cook for 3-4 minutes, or until translucent.

2. Add wine and cook until reduced by three-quarters.

3. Remove pan from heat and add butter cubes one at a time, whisking until completely melted. Add parsley and season to taste with pepper.

4. Serve immediately, using the Beurre Blanc as a dipping sauce for the crab legs. Makes 4 servings.

Tip: As a variation, add red pepper flakes to the sauce for color and heat.

When you can't catch your own.™

Crab Scampi
PHILLIPS

2 tablespoons olive oil
2 tablespoons margarine, soft tub
2 tablespoons chopped garlic
2/3 cup dry white wine
4 teaspoons Worcestershire sauce
2 tablespoons fresh lemon juice
1/4 teaspoon red pepper flakes
1/4 cup canned or bottled clam juice
1 pound Phillips* Crab Meat
2 teaspoons chopped fresh parsley
Salt and pepper
8 ounces dried spinach-flavored pasta (such as fettuccine), cooked until al dente and drained

1. Heat oil and margarine in a large skillet over medium heat. Add garlic and cook until lightly browned.

2. Add wine, Worcestershire sauce, lemon juice, red pepper flakes and clam juice. Bring to a boil and cook for 4 minutes, or until slightly reduced.

3. Gently stir in crab meat and parsley. Add salt and pepper to taste.

4. Serve crab mixture over spinach pasta. Makes 4 servings.

* Brands may vary by region; substitute a similar product.

Mary O's Marinated Dungeness Crab Legs
PACIFIC SEAFOOD ▼

2 large Pacific Seafood cooked Dungeness crabs
1/4 **cup extra-virgin olive oil**
1/4 **cup red wine vinegar**
1/2 **teaspoon garlic powder**
1/4 **teaspoon ground black pepper**
1/4 **teaspoon salt**

1. Clean and wash crabs. Separate the legs, keeping the shoulder attached to each leg. On a cutting board, crack each segment of the legs by gently tapping with the handle of a butter knife or a small rubber mallet. Place the cracked legs in a large bowl.

2. Pour olive oil over crab legs.

3. Mix remaining ingredients well. Pour mixture over crab legs and gently toss to coat evenly. Refrigerate for at least 3 hours and up to 12 hours, tossing once an hour.

4. Serve with bread, salad and your favorite beverage. Makes 2 servings.

Shrimp Scampi with Angel Hair Pasta
GOLD-N-SOFT ▲

8 ounces Gold-N-Soft* Margarine
4 garlic cloves, chopped
1 tablespoon chopped fresh oregano
1 tablespoon chopped fresh basil
1 1/2 teaspoons chopped fresh parsley
1/8 teaspoon salt
1 1/2 pounds medium shrimp, peeled and deveined
1/2 cup dry white wine
Juice of 1 lemon
8 cherry tomatoes, halved
1 pound angel hair pasta, cooked until al dente and drained

1. Combine margarine, garlic, oregano, basil, parsley and salt in a sauté pan and warm over low heat until margarine has melted.

2. Increase heat to medium-high, add shrimp to the pan and sauté.

3. When shrimp is half done (about 4 minutes), add wine and lemon juice; sauté for another 3 minutes.

4. Add tomatoes and reduce heat to low.

5. Mix in hot cooked pasta and cook for an additional 3 minutes. Serve immediately. Makes 4 servings.

Brands may vary by region; substitute a similar product.

◢◤ Ventura Foods LLC

Citrus Salad with Grilled Shrimp Adobo
SEALD SWEET ▲

MARINADE
4 garlic cloves, minced
1 teaspoon ground cumin
1/2 cup fresh-squeezed grapefruit juice
1/4 cup fresh-squeezed orange juice
2 tablespoons extra-virgin olive oil
Salt and pepper

1 pound jumbo shrimp, peeled, deveined, tails on
4 fresh Seald Sweet* oranges
4 fresh Seald Sweet* grapefruit
5 cups spinach leaves or romaine lettuce

1. To prepare marinade, combine garlic, cumin, grapefruit juice, orange juice and olive oil in a blender and process until smooth. Add salt and pepper to taste.

2. Combine shrimp in a bowl with two-thirds of marinade. Stir to mix. Cover and marinate shrimp for 30 minutes, turning occasionally.

3. Cut the rind (both zest and white pith) off the fruit. Make V-shaped cuts to remove segments from membranes, working over a bowl to catch juice. Remove seeds. Alternate orange and grapefruit segments around the edge of a platter. Mound spinach or lettuce in the center.

4. Preheat barbecue grill or broiler to high. Grill or broil shrimp 1-2 minutes per side. Arrange shrimp on top of the salad. Spoon reserved marinade over greens, citrus and shrimp. Makes 4 servings.

Recipe created by Steven Raichlen.
Brands may vary by region; substitute a similar product.

Seald ❂ Sweet®
INTERNATIONAL

Shrimp Scampi Fettuccine with Asparagus and Red Bell Pepper
SeaPak ▲

8 ounces SeaPak* Shrimp Scampi
2 cups fresh asparagus tips (top 4 inches of stalk)
1 cup thinly sliced red bell pepper
2 cups cooked fettuccine

1. Prepare Shrimp Scampi according to the sauté directions on the package, sautéing for 5 minutes.
2. After 5 minutes of sautéing, add asparagus and red bell pepper. Continue to sauté the mixture over medium heat for 4-5 minutes.
3. Remove from the heat and toss with cooked fettuccine.
Makes 2 servings.

Brands may vary by region; substitute a similar product.

Coconut Shrimp with Mustard Balsamic Vinaigrette
MARGARITAVILLE SHRIMP ▲

1/3 cup Dijon mustard
1 1/2 cups prepared balsamic dressing
1 2-pound package Margaritaville* Calypso Coconut Shrimp
12 cups blended salad mix
1 pint cherry tomatoes, cut in half
36 snap peas or snow peas (1/3 pound), cut in half
1 1/2 cups diced red and green bell peppers
3/4 cup toasted sliced almonds (optional)
1/3 cup toasted shredded coconut (optional)

1. Mix mustard with balsamic dressing; set aside.
2. Prepare shrimp according to package directions.
3. Place cooked shrimp and vegetables in a large salad bowl and toss gently with vinaigrette to taste.
4. Sprinkle with almonds and coconut, if desired. Serve immediately.
Makes 6 servings.

Brands may vary by region; substitute a similar product.

Entrées

Salmone Modena
AquaChile

4 6-ounce fresh skinless AquaChile Atlantic salmon fillets
Salt
Pepper
5 ounces butter
2 tablespoons finely diced red onion
1 cup balsamic vinegar of Modena

1. Sprinkle salmon with salt and pepper to taste.

2. Grill on aluminum foil for 3 minutes on each side, or until cooked to taste.

3. Meanwhile, melt a small amount of the butter over medium heat in a sauté pan. Add red onion and cook until it becomes translucent.

4. Add vinegar and cook until it is reduced by two-thirds.

5. Cut remaining butter into pieces and add gradually to the sauce, stirring until completely melted.

6. Place grilled salmon on plates and serve with the sauce.

Makes 4 servings.

Tip: Serve with sautéed portobello mushrooms, sautéed spinach and shrimp risotto.

Salmon Fillets à la Blanc
FJORD SEAFOOD ▼

1 pound fresh Kirkland Signature salmon fillets
Salt
Pepper
1 cup diced tomatoes
¼ cup Cabernet Sauvignon Blanc or other dry white wine
¾ teaspoon dried basil
¼ cup shredded Swiss cheese

1. Preheat oven to 350°F.
2. Cover a baking pan with aluminum foil.
3. Place salmon fillets in the pan and sprinkle with salt and pepper to taste. Cover with diced tomatoes. Pour wine over salmon. Sprinkle evenly with basil.
4. Bake for 15 minutes. Remove pan from the oven and quickly sprinkle cheese over salmon. Bake for an additional 3-5 minutes, or until cheese is melted and salmon is cooked to taste. Makes 2-3 servings.

Fjord Seafood USA

Southwest Stuffed Salmon with Chipotle-Lime Aioli
FISH HOUSE FOODS

3 Roma tomatoes, halved
4 tablespoons olive oil, divided
Salt and pepper
3 portions Kirkland Signature stuffed salmon entrée
1/2 garlic clove, minced
12 ounces fresh spinach

CHIPOTLE-LIME AIOLI
1 cup mayonnaise
1 tablespoon chipotle puree
2 tablespoons water
Juice of 1/2 lime
1 garlic clove, minced
1/2 teaspoon minced fresh cilantro
Pinch of salt

1. Preheat oven to 400°F.
2. Prepare Chipotle-Lime Aioli: In a bowl, combine mayonnaise, chipotle puree, water, lime juice, garlic, cilantro and salt.
3. Coat tomatoes with 2 tablespoons olive oil and place cut side down on a sheet pan. Sprinkle with salt and pepper to taste. Bake for 30 minutes, or until browned.
4. Bake stuffed salmon for about 30 minutes, following package directions.
5. Heat 2 tablespoons olive oil in a sauté pan over high heat. Add garlic and sauté for 20 seconds. Add spinach and sauté until wilted. Season to taste.
6. Place spinach on plates, top with salmon and drizzle with aioli. Place 2 roasted tomato halves on each plate. Makes 3 servings.

FISH HOUSE FOODS, INC.
VISTA, CA 92083

Salmon Newburg
SMOKI FOODS

1 tablespoon olive oil
1 1/2 pounds fresh Kirkland Signature* skinless, boneless salmon
1/4 cup butter
1 12-ounce can evaporated milk
1 egg yolk, beaten
1 tablespoon crushed dried basil leaves or 3 tablespoons chopped fresh basil

1 tablespoon lemon juice
1 teaspoon seasoning salt
8 ounces cream cheese
1 cup shredded Colby Jack cheese
1 cup shredded sharp Cheddar cheese
2 cups of your favorite rice, cooked
Paprika

1. Heat oil in a skillet over high heat. Add salmon and cook until browned and just opaque in the center.
2. In a double boiler, combine butter, evaporated milk, egg yolk, basil, lemon juice, seasoning salt, cream cheese, Colby Jack and Cheddar. Cook, stirring constantly, over medium heat (do not boil) until the sauce simmers and is creamy.
3. Add bite-size pieces of salmon to simmering sauce.
4. Place cooked rice on plates and top with salmon and sauce. Sprinkle with paprika. Makes 6 servings.

Variations: Add sautéed sweet onions, sautéed button mushrooms, cooked shrimp or prawns, sautéed scallops or tuna, or all of the above.

* Brands may vary by region; substitute a similar product.

SMOKI FOODS

Salmon and Pasta with Dill Cheddar Sauce
TILLAMOOK CHEESE ▼

1 pound center-cut salmon fillet with skin
1 cup white wine or water
Salt and pepper
1/2 pound asparagus spears, trimmed and cut into 1-inch pieces
1 cup shelled fresh or frozen peas
8 ounces dried fettuccine
2 tablespoons butter
1/4 cup minced shallots
1 1/4 cups whipping cream
2 teaspoons minced fresh dill
8 ounces (2 cups) shredded Tillamook* Vintage White Extra Sharp Cheddar Cheese or Tillamook* Sharp Cheddar Cheese

1. Preheat oven to 350°F.
2. Place salmon in an 8-inch baking dish with wine or water and salt and pepper to taste. Cover with foil, place in the oven, and poach until cooked through, about 20 minutes. Remove skin and flake salmon into 1-inch pieces.
3. Cook asparagus and peas in boiling water until crisp-tender, 3 minutes. Drain and place in ice water to stop cooking; drain.
4. Cook pasta according to package directions; drain and keep warm.
5. Melt butter in a large skillet over medium heat. Add shallots and sauté until softened, 5 minutes. Add cream and 1 teaspoon dill; bring to a boil, stirring frequently. Boil, uncovered, until reduced to 1 cup. Stir in 1 1/2 cups cheese and remaining dill. Add salmon, asparagus and peas; cook, stirring gently, until cheese melts and salmon is hot, 2-3 minutes. Season to taste with salt and pepper.
6. Toss sauce with pasta. Sprinkle each serving with grated cheese.
Makes 4-6 servings.

Brands may vary by region; substitute a similar product.

Salmon Baked in Parchment
AQUAFARMS ▼

Parchment paper
1 4 1/2-ounce package long-grain and wild rice mix
1 small zucchini
1 medium carrot
4 Aquafarms* skinless salmon fillets
1 tablespoon olive oil

CITRUS BASIL RUB
1 tablespoon chopped lemon peel
2 garlic cloves, pressed
1 tablespoon chopped fresh basil
1 teaspoon salt
1 teaspoon lemon pepper

1. Preheat oven to 425°F. Cut four 15-inch squares of parchment paper. Fold in half and cut to make large heart shapes when unfolded.

2. Prepare rice mix according to package directions. Slice zucchini and carrot into strips.

3. To prepare the rub, combine all ingredients in a small bowl.

4. For each serving, open a paper heart and spoon 1/2 cup of the rice mixture onto the right side; top with 3-4 pieces each of zucchini and carrot. Top with salmon fillet. Drizzle salmon with olive oil and sprinkle with 1/2 tablespoon of the rub, covering the entire fillet.

5. Fold the left side of the heart over the salmon. Starting at the top, tightly seal the packet by making a series of short, narrow overlapping folds along the open edge. Twist the bottom tip and turn up.

6. Arrange packets on a cookie sheet or 10-by-15-by-1-inch pan. Bake for 13-15 minutes. Carefully open a packet to test that salmon flakes easily with a fork. To serve, cut an X through the top layer of paper and fold back the points. Makes 4 servings.

* Brands may vary by region; substitute a similar product.

"In a Heartbeat" Orange/Ginger Salmon
CAMANCHACA ▼

1 orange
4-inch piece fresh ginger, peeled and grated
2 tablespoons olive oil
2 tablespoons honey
¼ cup orange liqueur (Cointreau or Grand Marnier)
4 6-ounce fresh skinless, boneless Camanchaca* salmon portions
Salt and pepper to taste

1. Preheat oven to 400°F.
2. Grate the peel of the orange, then remove the peel and slice the fruit.

3. In a small bowl, combine grated orange peel, ginger, olive oil, honey and orange liqueur.
4. Place salmon in a baking dish and season with salt and pepper. Spread the sauce over the salmon.
5. Place on lower rack of the oven and bake, uncovered, for approximately 12 minutes, or until cooked to taste. Baste salmon with pan juices for approximately 6 minutes.
6. Garnish salmon with orange slices. Serve with a choice of steamed vegetables and long-grain brown rice. Makes 4 servings.

Brands may vary by region; substitute a similar product.

Grilled Salmon with Emerald Kiwifruit Salsa
AQUAGOLD SEAFOOD ▲

3 tablespoons maple syrup or honey
1 tablespoon Chesapeake Bay-style seafood seasoning
4 6-ounce boneless, skinless fresh Atlantic salmon fillets

EMERALD KIWIFRUIT SALSA
2 large kiwis, peeled and cut into 1/4-inch dice (1 cup)
2 tablespoons finely chopped shallots or red onion
1 serrano or small jalapeño chile, seeded and minced
1 tablespoon minced fresh cilantro
1-2 teaspoons maple syrup or honey
1/2 teaspoon Chesapeake Bay-style seafood seasoning (or to taste)

1. Preheat indoor countertop nonstick grill or "fire up" outdoor grill.
2. In a small bowl, combine maple syrup and Chesapeake Bay seasoning. Lightly brush on both sides of salmon.
3. Prepare Emerald Kiwifruit Salsa: Combine kiwis, shallots, chile and cilantro. Taste before adding just enough maple syrup to soften any harsh tartness. Gradually add Chesapeake Bay seasoning to taste. Serve at room temperature or chilled.
4. Grill salmon just until done. For 1-inch-thick fillets, allow about 5 minutes on indoor grill. On outdoor grill, turn salmon after 4 minutes; grill second side, checking for doneness after 4 minutes.
5. Serve salmon with salsa. Makes 4 servings.

Hapa Haole Ahi
T.J. KRAFT ▲

1 1/2 tablespoons dry English mustard
1 1/2 tablespoons warm water
1 tablespoon soy sauce
1 cup white wine
1/4 cup white wine vinegar
3 tablespoons minced shallots
3 tablespoons crushed white peppercorns
1/2 cup heavy cream
1/2 pound unsalted butter, room temperature, cut into 1/2-inch cubes
8 T.J. Kraft* ahi tuna steaks
Salt and pepper

1. In a small bowl, mix dry mustard, water and soy sauce; set aside.
2. Place wine, vinegar, shallots and peppercorns in a saucepan and cook over medium heat until liquid has evaporated. Add cream and heat gently until it simmers. Gradually stir in butter.
3. Add mustard/soy mixture to the sauce; strain.
4. Season ahi steaks with salt and pepper to taste.
5. Heat a skillet over high heat. Sear ahi for 2 minutes per side for rare. If you prefer it more well done, place the seared ahi in a preheated 400°F oven for another 5-7 minutes.
6. Place ahi on plates and serve with sauce. Makes 8 servings.

* Brands may vary by region; substitute a similar product.

Sesame-Crusted Grilled Ahi Tuna in Ginger Soy Marinade
WESTERN UNITED FISH COMPANY ▼

1 cup soy sauce
1 teaspoon sesame oil
1 tablespoon grated fresh ginger
5 garlic cloves, minced
1/2 cup packed light brown sugar
1/2 cup orange juice
2 fresh Western United Fish Company* ahi tuna steaks
Sesame seeds
Canola oil

1. Mix soy sauce, sesame oil, ginger, garlic, brown sugar and orange juice together for the marinade.
2. Place ahi in the marinade for at least 30 minutes.
3. Remove ahi from the marinade and sprinkle with sesame seeds.
4. Brush grill with canola oil. Grill ahi over hot coals for 3 minutes per side, or until it is seared. Makes 2 servings.

To serve with grilled vegetables: Prepare sweet potato, eggplant, red bell pepper, zucchini, red onion and asparagus spears for grilling. Brush with olive oil, sprinkle with salt and a dash of pepper, and grill.

Brands may vary by region; substitute a similar product.

Western United Fish Company
Your Direct Source

Lemon Caper Sole
NORTH COAST SEAFOODS ▲

1 cup flour

2 teaspoons kosher salt

1 teaspoon ground pepper

2 tablespoons olive oil, divided

8 2- to 4-ounce North Coast Seafoods* sole fillets

1/2 cup diced white onion

1 teaspoon chopped garlic

1/2 cup white wine

Juice of 2 lemons

3 tablespoons capers

2 tablespoons chopped fresh parsley

4 tablespoons butter, cut into 1/2-inch cubes

1. Preheat oven to 250°F.

2. Season flour with salt and pepper.

3. Heat 1 tablespoon oil in a large sauté pan over medium heat. Dredge sole fillets in flour, shake off excess and place 1 or 2 in the pan. Cook for 2 minutes on each side, then transfer to the oven to keep warm. Repeat with remaining fillets.

4. Wipe any flour from the pan. Return pan to high heat and add 1 tablespoon oil. Add onion and garlic; sauté until soft. Stir in wine, lemon juice and capers; cook to reduce by a third. Turn off heat, add parsley and gradually whisk in butter.

5. Serve sole fillets with sauce. Makes 4 servings.

Brands may vary by region; substitute a similar product.

Pan-Fried Almond &
Parmesan-Crusted Flounder
SOUSA SEAFOOD ▲

2 large eggs

1 1/2 cups all-purpose flour

Kosher salt

Ground black pepper

1 1/2 pounds fresh flounder fillets, split lengthwise

3 tablespoons olive oil

3 tablespoons unsalted butter

Lemon wedges and fresh parsley sprigs, for garnish

ALMOND & PARMESAN BREAD CRUMBS

1/2 cup coarsely chopped sliced almonds

1/2 cup grated Parmigiano-Reggiano cheese

1/2 cup fresh white bread crumbs

2 tablespoons minced Italian parsley

1/2 teaspoon kosher salt

1/4 teaspoon ground black pepper

1. Prepare Almond & Parmesan Bread Crumbs: Combine all ingredients in a large shallow bowl.

2. Crack eggs into a large shallow bowl and beat well with 2 teaspoons water. Place flour in another large shallow bowl.

3. Preheat a 12-inch skillet over medium heat.

4. Lightly salt and pepper the flounder fillets. Dredge in flour, dip in egg wash and coat with Almond & Parmesan Bread Crumbs.

5. Add olive oil and butter to the skillet. Add fillets and cook for 1 1/2-2 minutes on each side, or until crisp and golden brown. Garnish with lemon wedges and parsley sprigs. Makes 4 servings.

Recipe provided by Jasper White, Shore Food, ©2005, W.W. Norton.

Tuscan Cod
TRIDENT SEAFOODS ▾

4 Trident Seafoods Premium Cod frozen fillet portions
Salt
Freshly ground black pepper
2 tablespoons chopped fresh basil
8 slices tomato
4 slices fresh mozzarella
1 cup seasoned bread crumbs
1 tablespoon chopped fresh parsley
¹/₂ tablespoon chopped fresh garlic
1 ¹/₂ tablespoons olive oil
Seasonal mixed salad greens

1. Preheat oven to 425°F.

2. Place frozen cod fillets in a lightly oiled ovenproof dish. Season to taste with salt and pepper, then sprinkle with basil. Overlapping slightly, arrange in sequence on each fillet 1 slice of tomato, then 1 mozzarella slice, then another slice of tomato.

3. In a small bowl, combine bread crumbs, parsley, garlic and olive oil. Spoon crumb mixture over fillets.

4. Bake for 30-35 minutes. If desired, broil for 30 seconds to further crisp the crumb topping.

5. Serve each crumb-topped cod fillet on a bed of seasonal mixed salad greens. Makes 4 servings.

Dijon Tilapia Fillets
MOUNTAIN STREAM ▲

2 tablespoons butter
1 tablespoon Dijon mustard
1 teaspoon Worcestershire sauce
1 1/2 tablespoons fresh lemon juice
4 Mountain Stream* tilapia fillets
Salt and pepper
3 tablespoons fresh bread crumbs
Chopped fresh parsley, for garnish

1. Preheat oven to 450°F.
2. In a medium saucepan, melt butter over low heat. Add mustard, Worcestershire sauce and lemon juice and mix well.
3. Season tilapia fillets with salt and pepper to taste. Place in a lightly greased baking pan, leaving space between fillets. Pour the sauce over the fillets and sprinkle with bread crumbs.
4. Bake for 7-8 minutes, or until just cooked through. Garnish with parsley and serve immediately. Makes 4 servings.

Brands may vary by region; substitute a similar product.

Tilapia Tacos
RIO MAR ▲

2 Rio Mar* fresh tilapia fillets
1 teaspoon taco seasoning
1 tablespoon vegetable oil
4 flour tortillas
1 cup prepared guacamole or your favorite recipe
4 hard taco shells
1/2 cup ranch dressing flavored with 1 teaspoon ground cumin
1 cup shredded cabbage
1/2 cup chipotle salsa

1. Sprinkle tilapia with taco seasoning. Heat oil in a large sauté pan over medium-high heat and cook fillets until they flake easily; leave whole or cut into strips.
2. Spread each tortilla evenly with guacamole and wrap around a taco shell. Place several strips of warm cooked tilapia in the shell and top with 1 tablespoon ranch dressing.
3. Top with shredded cabbage and 1 tablespoon chipotle salsa. Serve immediately, with remaining toppings to be added at the table, if desired. Makes 4 servings.

Brands may vary by region; substitute a similar product.

Pesto Tilapia
RAIN FOREST AQUACULTURE ▲

2 ounces white wine
2 5- to 7-ounce Rain Forest* fresh tilapia fillets
6 ounces prepared pesto sauce
1 pint heavy whipping cream
1 tablespoon butter
Salt and pepper

1. Heat wine in a sauté pan until it just begins to bubble. Add tilapia and cook over medium heat until it is just cooked through.

2. Add pesto sauce, cream and butter to the pan. Simmer until the sauce thickens. Season to taste with salt and pepper.

3. Serve immediately. Makes 2 servings.

Brands may vary by region; substitute a similar product.

Coconut Fried Tilapia Fingers with Mango Ginger Sauce
REGAL SPRINGS ▲

4 cups cornflakes, crushed
1 1/2 cups flaked coconut
2 eggs
Splash of milk
Salt, pepper and paprika to taste
4 6-ounce Regal Springs* tilapia fillets, cut into 1-ounce fingers
2 cups all-purpose flour
Vegetable oil

MANGO GINGER SAUCE
1 ripe mango, peeled, chopped

and pureed
1 teaspoon grated fresh ginger
1/4 cup cider vinegar
1 cup orange juice
1 teaspoon Thai sambal oelek or 1/2 teaspoon cayenne pepper
1/2 cup white wine
1/2 cup granulated sugar
2 tablespoons cornstarch dissolved in 2 tablespoons cold water

1. Prepare Mango Ginger Sauce: Place first 7 ingredients in a saucepan and bring to a boil. Whisk in cornstarch slowly. Serve warm or at room temperature.

2. Combine crushed cornflakes and coconut.

3. In a bowl, whisk together eggs, milk, salt, pepper and paprika.

4. Dust tilapia with flour. Dip in egg wash. Coat in cornflake/coconut blend, then set aside on a cookie sheet.

5. Heat 1 inch of oil in a large heavy skillet over medium-high heat to 375°F (about 5 minutes). Fry tilapia in batches until golden brown.

6. Serve with Mango Ginger Sauce. Makes 4 servings.

Tip: Serve with rice and Asian vegetables, or as an appetizer.

Brands may vary by region; substitute a similar product.

Rainbow Trout with Shrimp Cornbread Stuffing
IDAHO TROUT COMPANY ▲

1 8 1/2-ounce package
   Jiffy corn muffins

1 egg

1/3 cup milk

1/2 cup chicken stock

1 teaspoon chopped garlic

1/4 cup chopped yellow onion

1/4 cup diced celery

1/2 teaspoon dried summer savory

Pinch of thyme, chopped

2 tablespoons butter, plus
   2 tablespoons melted butter

2 tablespoons chopped
   red bell pepper

1 tablespoon chopped
   black olives

1/4 cup dry wheat bread
   cut in 1/4-inch cubes

2 tablespoons chopped fresh parsley

1/4 cup thinly sliced green onion

1/4 cup bay shrimp (optional)

Salt and pepper to taste

6 Idaho Trout* whole dressed
   rainbow trout

1. Preheat oven to 350°F.

2. Combine corn muffin mix, egg and milk. Pour into greased
9-by-11-inch pan and bake for 20 minutes. Let cool.

3. Simmer chicken stock, garlic, yellow onion, celery, savory, thyme
and 2 tablespoons butter in a saucepan until vegetables are translucent,
about 3 minutes.

4. Crumble cornbread into a bowl. Fold in chicken stock mixture, bell pepper,
olives, bread cubes, parsley, green onion, shrimp, and salt and pepper; chill.

5. Fill trout with stuffing; brush with melted butter. Bake for 14 minutes,
or until fish is opaque and stuffing is hot. Makes 6 servings.

Brands may vary by region; substitute a similar product.

Rainbow Trout Adobo with Corn Salsa
CLEAR SPRINGS ▲

2 cups dry white wine

1/4 cup lime juice

2 tablespoons canned chopped
   chiles in adobo sauce

1 teaspoon chopped garlic

1 whole Clear Springs*
   rainbow trout

Butter

1 bunch baby spinach

CORN SALSA

1/3 cup corn kernels

2 tablespoons diced green chiles

2 tablespoons diced red onion

1/3 cup diced tomato

1 teaspoon fresh lemon juice

1/4 cup chopped fresh cilantro

1 tablespoon prepared adobo sauce

1/2 teaspoon sea salt

1. Combine wine, lime juice, chiles in adobo sauce and garlic. Pour over
trout and marinate in the refrigerator for 2 hours; remove and pat dry.

2. Preheat oven to 400°F. Place the fish in a buttered baking dish and dot
with butter.

3. Bake for 13-15 minutes, or until just cooked through.

4. Prepare Corn Salsa: Combine all ingredients in a saucepan and heat
until warm.

5. Place baby spinach on a platter, top with the fish and spoon on Corn Salsa.
Makes 4 servings.

Brands may vary by region; substitute a similar product.

CLEAR
SPRINGS
FOODS®

Sautéed Catfish with Sliced Lettuce Niçoise
DELTA PRIDE ▼

2 tablespoons olive oil

1 teaspoon chopped
   fresh rosemary

1 teaspoon harissa or chopped
   fresh chile

1 teaspoon chopped garlic

4 6-ounce Delta Pride
   catfish fillets

Salt

1 head iceberg lettuce, cut in
   4 flat circles

1 cup French green beans,
   blanched in salted water

VINAIGRETTE

1 tablespoon red wine vinegar

3 tablespoons warm water

Salt

3 tablespoons olive oil

2 tablespoons chopped
   kalamata olives

1 tomato, seeded and diced

4 basil leaves, minced

2 hard-boiled eggs, chopped

1. Mix olive oil, rosemary, harissa and garlic. Add catfish and marinate for 1 hour.

2. Heat a medium sauté pan over medium heat. Season catfish with salt to taste and cook until golden brown and fish flakes with a fork; set aside.

3. To prepare the vinaigrette, combine vinegar, water and salt to taste in a small bowl. Whisk in olive oil gradually. Stir in olives, tomato, basil and chopped eggs.

4. Place lettuce circles on plates and arrange green beans on top. Drizzle with vinaigrette and then top with fish fillets. Add a bit more vinaigrette and serve immediately. Makes 4 servings.

Recipe by Master Chef Jose Gutierrez, Memphis, Tennessee

Entrées I

Garlic-Studded Bone-in Prime Rib
BRAWLEY BEEF

1 Brawley Beef* bone-in prime rib
10 garlic cloves, peeled and quartered
1/2 cup oil
1/4 cup fresh rosemary leaves
1/4 cup fresh thyme leaves
1/2 cup Dijon mustard
Coarse salt
Black pepper
2 pounds shallots
2 pounds carrots
2 pounds celery
1 bottle red wine
2 quarts beef broth

1. Preheat oven to 300°F.
2. With a small knife, cut about 10 slits in the prime rib. Stuff each cut with pieces of garlic.

3. In a small bowl, combine oil, rosemary, thyme and mustard; rub over the meat. Sprinkle generously with salt and pepper.
4. Roughly chop vegetables and place in a roasting pan to make a "rack." Place the rib on the vegetables and roast in the oven for approximately 12-15 minutes per pound, or to an internal temperature of about 115°F (for medium rare).
5. Remove meat from the pan and let rest for 15-20 minutes; this allows the juices to spread back through the entire roast.
6. Add wine to the roasting pan and cook on the stovetop over medium heat until almost dry. Add beef broth and cook to reduce by about half. Strain sauce, adjust seasoning and serve over well-rested prime rib.
Makes 8-10 servings.

Recipe created by Mark Ayers, executive chef, California Market/Highlands Inn, Carmel, California.
* Brands may vary by region; substitute a similar product.

BRAWLEY BEEF

Beef Steaks with Parmesan-Grilled Vegetables
TYSON ▲

1 tablespoon minced garlic

2 teaspoons dried basil

1 teaspoon ground black pepper

2 beef porterhouse steaks (about 2 pounds), or 2 beef T-bone steaks (about 2 pounds)

1/4 cup grated Parmesan cheese

2 tablespoons olive oil

2 tablespoons red wine vinegar

2 medium red bell peppers, quartered

1 large red onion, sliced 1/2 inch thick

1. Preheat grill to medium.

2. Wash hands. Combine garlic, basil and pepper in a small bowl. Remove 4 teaspoons and press onto steaks. Wash hands.

3. Add Parmesan, olive oil and vinegar to remaining seasoning and mix well.

4. Place steaks in the center of the cooking grid; arrange vegetables around steaks. Grill steaks, uncovered and turning occasionally, for 14-16 minutes for medium-rare to medium (internal temperature 150-160°F).

5. Grill bell peppers for 12-15 minutes and onion for 15-20 minutes, or until tender, turning once. Brush vegetables with seasoning mixture during last 10 minutes. Makes 4 servings.

Tip: To broil, place steaks and vegetables 3-4 inches from heat. Broil, turning once, 15-20 minutes. Brush vegetables with seasoning mixture during last 3-4 minutes.

Eye of Round with Roasted Vegetables
REYNOLDS ▲

Reynolds Wrap Heavy Duty Aluminum Foil

1 eye of round beef roast (2-2 1/2 pounds)

2 garlic cloves, minced

2 tablespoons olive oil

2 tablespoons fresh lemon juice

2 teaspoons beef seasoning for grilling or garlic pepper seasoning

2 teaspoons dried Italian seasoning

1/2 teaspoon seasoned salt

2 cups peeled baby carrots

2 large zucchini, cut in 1/2-inch slices

2 large yellow squash, cut in 1/2-inch slices

1 medium red bell pepper, cut in 1/2-inch slices

1. Preheat oven to 325°F. For easy cleanup, line a 9-by-13-by-2-inch pan with foil.

2. Place beef in the pan. In a small bowl, combine garlic, olive oil and lemon juice. Brush beef with about 1/4 of mixture. Sprinkle beef with beef seasoning for grilling.

3. Add Italian seasoning and seasoned salt to remaining olive oil mixture. Place vegetables in a large bowl, add olive oil mixture and toss to coat. Arrange vegetables around beef.

4. Bake for 1 1/4-1 1/2 hours, or until a meat thermometer reads 135°F. Transfer meat to a cutting board; tent with foil. Let stand for 10-15 minutes (temperature will rise to about 145°F, for medium-rare). Makes 6-8 servings.

Reynolds Kitchens Tip: To line the pan, flip it upside down. Press a sheet of foil around pan. Remove foil. Flip pan upright and drop foil inside. Crimp edges to the rim.

Entrées ▎

Chef Brando's Beef Bourguignon
SMITHFIELD BEEF GROUP ▲

Vegetable oil spray
1 teaspoon olive oil
5 medium onions, sliced (5 cups)
2 pounds lean top sirloin roast (or other lean cut),
    cut into 1-inch cubes
1 1/2 tablespoons all-purpose flour
1/2 teaspoon dried marjoram, crumbled
1/4 teaspoon dried thyme, crumbled
Freshly ground black pepper
1 1/4 cups dry red wine
3/4 cup low-sodium beef broth
1/2 pound fresh mushrooms, sliced (3-3 1/2 cups)

1. Lightly coat a large heavy skillet with vegetable oil spray. Add olive oil
and heat over medium-high heat. Sauté onions until translucent, 2-3
minutes; remove and set aside.
2. Add beef to the skillet and sauté until browned, 10-12 minutes.
Sprinkle with flour, marjoram, thyme and pepper to taste; stir to mix well.
3. Stir in wine and broth. Reduce heat, cover and simmer for 1 1/2-2 hours,
or until almost tender. Add more wine and broth (2 parts wine to 1 part
broth) as necessary to keep beef barely covered.
4. Return onions to the skillet and add mushrooms. Cover and simmer,
stirring occasionally, for 30 minutes, or until beef is tender and sauce
has thickened.
5. Serve over rice or noodles. Makes 6 servings.

Tip: This tastes best when made ahead so the flavors have time to mingle.

Pork Tenderloins in Maple Sauce
OLD FASHIONED MAPLE CREST ▲

12 slices pork tenderloin, 2 ounces each
Salt and pepper
1/4 cup butter
2/3 cup apple cider
1/3 cup Old Fashioned Maple Crest* 100% pure maple syrup
1 cup beef bouillon
2 teaspoons cornstarch
2 tablespoons cold butter

1. Slightly flatten pork slices to 1/2-inch thickness. Season with salt and
pepper to taste.
2. Melt 1/4 cup butter in a sauté pan over high heat. Add pork slices
and sear. Reduce heat and finish cooking (about 5 minutes).
Remove meat from the pan.
3. Add cider to the pan and cook over high heat, stirring to dissolve
concentrated juices. Add maple syrup and boil to reduce by half.
4. Combine beef bouillon and cornstarch. Add thickened beef bouillon to
the pan, cook to reduce slightly, and check seasoning.
5. Finish sauce by adding pieces of cold butter, whisking until smooth.
Remove immediately from heat and reheat pork in the sauce off the stove.
Serve at once. Makes 6 servings.

* Brands may vary by region; substitute a similar product.

Classic Baby Back Ribs
CATTLEMEN'S ▲

3-4 pounds pork baby back ribs (2-3 racks)
1 cup Cattlemen's* Barbecue Sauce

RUB
1 tablespoon garlic powder
1 tablespoon onion powder
1 tablespoon salt
1 tablespoon dry mustard
1 tablespoon ground black pepper
1 tablespoon ground white pepper
1 cup packed brown sugar
1/2 cup paprika

1. The night before cooking the ribs, prepare and apply the rub. Simply mix all the rub ingredients together. Rub mixture all over the ribs, then wrap them in heavy plastic wrap and refrigerate overnight.
2. Grill ribs over indirect heat on a covered grill for 90 minutes (or in a 350°F oven).
3. Baste with barbecue sauce and cook 30 minutes longer, or until the meat is very tender. Makes 4 servings.

* Brands may vary by region; substitute a similar product.

Grilled Veal Chops with Sage Jus
WOLVERINE PACKING ▲

1/4 cup olive oil
1/4 cup whole fresh sage leaves
4 garlic cloves, smashed
1 cup veal stock or beef broth
Salt and pepper
4 veal loin or rib chops, cut 1 inch thick

1. Combine olive oil, whole sage leaves and garlic in a small saucepan. Simmer over low heat for 30 minutes. Strain out solids. Set aside.
2. Bring stock to a boil in a saucepan over high heat. Lower heat to medium and simmer for 22-24 minutes, or until reduced by half. Add sage oil and simmer for 1 minute. Season to taste with salt and pepper. Set aside and keep warm.
3. Grill veal chops, uncovered, turning once, for 12-14 minutes, or until cooked to taste.
4. Serve each chop with 2 tablespoons sage jus. Makes 4 servings.

Veal Chops with Mustard Sage Sauce
PLUME DE VEAU ▼

1 ¹/₂ tablespoons butter
1 teaspoon vegetable oil
2 1-inch-thick Plume De Veau* veal chops (loin or rib)
Dried rubbed sage
Freshly ground black pepper
Fresh sage leaves, for garnish

MUSTARD SAGE SAUCE

2 ¹/₂ tablespoons chopped shallots
¹/₃ cup unsalted beef broth
2 tablespoons minced fresh sage or 2 teaspoons dried
    rubbed sage, divided
2 teaspoons Dijon mustard
¹/₄ cup half-and-half

1. Melt butter with oil in a heavy medium skillet over medium-high heat. Sprinkle chops with dried sage and pepper to taste. Add to the skillet and cook until browned, about 5 minutes per side.

2. Reduce heat to medium and cook to desired doneness, about 1 minute per side for medium-rare. Transfer veal to a plate and keep warm.

3. Prepare Mustard Sage Sauce: Add shallots to the same skillet; cook and stir for 1 minute. Add broth, 1 tablespoon minced sage and mustard; boil until very thick, scraping up browned bits, about 4 minutes. Add half-and-half and boil until liquid thickens to a sauce consistency, about 1 minute. Mix in remaining 1 tablespoon minced sage and any juices exuded by veal. Adjust seasoning.

4. Place chops on plates. Spoon sauce over the chops and garnish with fresh sage leaves. Makes 2 servings.

Tip: Serve with roasted potatoes and sautéed green beans.

* Brands may vary by region; substitute a similar product.

Veal Stew
PLUME DE VEAU ▲

Extra-virgin olive oil
1 green bell pepper, sliced
2 onions, chopped
1 tablespoon chopped garlic
2 1/2 pounds Plume De Veau* veal for stew
1 28-ounce can crushed tomatoes
1/2 tablespoon freshly ground black pepper
1 tablespoon dried Italian seasoning
Salt

1. Cover the bottom of a stew pot with olive oil and heat over medium-high heat. Add bell pepper, onions and garlic; cook until they start to brown.

2. Add veal cubes and brown/sear.

3. When all veal pieces are almost golden brown, add tomatoes, black pepper, Italian seasoning and salt to taste. Cook over medium heat for 35-40 minutes, stirring occasionally.

4. Then cover and simmer on low heat for 1 1/2 hours, stirring occasionally. Taste and add more Italian seasoning and garlic, if desired. Makes 8 servings.

Brands may vary by region; substitute a similar product.

Veal Cutlet Cordon Bleu
PLUME DE VEAU ▲

8 thin Plume De Veau* veal cutlets
Salt and pepper
4 thin slices Swiss cheese
4 thin slices ham
Flour for dredging
3 eggs, beaten
1/2 cup dry bread crumbs
1/2 cup butter

1. Gently pound veal cutlets between sheets of plastic wrap to flatten. Season to taste with salt and pepper.

2. Place 1 slice of cheese and 1 slice of ham on each of 4 veal cutlets. Cover with remaining 4 cutlets. Pound the edges together.

3. Dip veal in flour, then egg, and then bread crumbs.

4. Melt butter in a sauté pan over medium-high heat. Add veal and cook for 8 minutes, or until just cooked through. Makes 4 servings.

Brands may vary by region; substitute a similar product.

Stir-Fried Lemon Chicken
SUNKIST ◀

$^1/_3$ cup fresh-squeezed Sunkist lemon juice (approx. 2 lemons), divided
2 teaspoons Asian sesame oil
$^1/_2$ cup plus 3 tablespoons vegetable oil
1 $^1/_2$ pounds boneless, skinless chicken breasts, cut in 2-by-$^1/_2$-by-$^1/_2$-inch strips
1 $^1/_2$ pounds Asian vegetable blend
2 $^1/_4$ cups chicken broth, divided
$^1/_4$ cup cornstarch
$^1/_2$ cup soy sauce, divided
$^1/_4$ cup sugar
$^1/_2$ cup Sunkist lemon pieces
2 cups steamed rice
$^1/_4$ cup green onion cut in $^1/_2$-inch diagonal slices
2 teaspoons sesame seeds

1. Combine 4 teaspoons lemon juice, sesame oil and $^1/_2$ cup vegetable oil to make marinade. Pour over chicken and marinate, refrigerated, for 1-4 hours.
2. Place 3 tablespoons vegetable oil in a wok and heat over medium-high heat until smoking. Add the marinated chicken strips and stir-fry for 1-2 minutes. Add Asian vegetables and stir-fry for 1-2 minutes, or until the chicken is done.
3. Combine $^1/_4$ cup chicken broth and cornstarch to make a slurry. Set aside.
4. Combine remaining chicken broth, remaining lemon juice, $^1/_4$ cup soy sauce and sugar. Add to the wok, bring to a boil and slowly stir in slurry to thicken sauce. Stir lemon pieces into the sauce and heat through, then remove wok from the heat.
5. Mound steamed rice in the center of each plate. Pour chicken over the rice and sprinkle with green onion and sesame seeds. Drizzle with remaining soy sauce. Serve immediately. Makes 4 servings.

Sunkist

Mushroom Chicken Cream Topping
GIORGIO FOODS ▲

2 tablespoons vegetable or canola oil
$^1/_2$ medium onion, cut in $^1/_2$-inch dice
1 fresh garlic clove, chopped
1 boneless, skinless chicken breast, cut horizontally into $^1/_2$-inch strips
2 4-ounce cans Giorgio, Penn Dutch or Brandywine* mushrooms
1 tablespoon cornstarch
$^1/_2$ cup heavy cream, half-and-half or milk
Salt and pepper
Grated Parmesan cheese
Parsley, for garnish

1. Heat oil in a medium to large sauté pan over medium-high heat. Sauté onion, garlic and chicken strips until lightly browned (2 minutes).
2. Add mushrooms with broth. Cook for 3-5 minutes, or until chicken is cooked through.
3. In a small bowl, add cornstarch to cream and stir until smooth. Stir into the chicken mixture. Bring to a boil and cook until the sauce thickens. Stir well, then lower heat and simmer for 2 minutes. Season to taste with salt and pepper.
4. Serve over rice, noodles or pasta. Sprinkle with Parmesan cheese and garnish with parsley. Makes 2 servings.

Brands may vary by region; substitute a similar product.

Giorgio

Pecan-Crusted Chicken
with Honey-Mustard Sauce
KRAFT ▲

1 packet Shake 'n Bake Extra Crispy Seasoned Coating Mix
1 cup finely chopped Planters pecans
1 egg
1 tablespoon water
6 boneless, skinless chicken breast halves (2 pounds)
1/3 cup Miracle Whip Dressing
1/3 cup Grey Poupon Honey Mustard

1. Preheat oven to 400°F.
2. Combine coating mix and pecans in a shallow dish or pie plate; set aside.
3. Beat egg with water in a separate shallow dish.
4. Dip chicken in egg mixture, then in pecan mixture, turning to evenly coat both sides. Place on a foil-covered baking sheet.
5. Bake for 18-20 minutes, or until chicken is cooked through.
6. Meanwhile, combine dressing and mustard. Serve chicken with sauce on the side. Makes 6 servings.

Balsamic Chicken and Pears
KIRKLAND SIGNATURE/TYSON ▲

2 ripe pears, cored and thinly sliced
1/2 cup thinly sliced red onion
1 tablespoon olive oil
1/2 teaspoon dried thyme
1/2 teaspoon salt
1/4 teaspoon pepper
4 Kirkland Signature Frozen Boneless, Skinless Chicken Breasts*, thawed
1 tablespoon balsamic vinegar
Sprig of sage (optional)

1. Preheat oven to 450°F.
2. Wash hands. Place pear and onion slices in a single layer in a 9-by-13-inch baking dish.
3. Combine olive oil, thyme, salt and pepper in a shallow bowl. Spoon half of mixture over pears and onions. Cover dish tightly with foil; bake for 10 minutes.
4. Meanwhile, place chicken in remaining seasoning mixture, turning to coat on all sides. Wash hands.
5. Uncover pear and onion slices; arrange chicken on top and drizzle with vinegar. Discard remaining oil mixture. Bake, uncovered, for 20 minutes, or until chicken is done (internal temperature 170°F). Garnish with sage, if desired. Makes 4 servings.

Tips: Serve with a crisp fresh salad. Refrigerate leftovers.

Brands may vary by region; substitute a similar product.

Black Forest Chicken Skillet
KIRKLAND SIGNATURE/TYSON ▲

4 Kirkland Signature Frozen Boneless, Skinless Chicken Breasts*, thawed
1 teaspoon seasoned salt
Cooking spray
1 small onion, chopped
3 medium potatoes, cut into 1/2-inch cubes (about 3 1/2 cups)
1/4 pound Continental Deli Black Forest Ham, cut into thin strips
3 cups cabbage slaw mix
1 teaspoon caraway seed, crushed

1. Wash hands. Sprinkle chicken with seasoned salt. Wash hands.
2. Spray a large nonstick skillet with cooking spray and heat to medium-high. Add chicken, cover and cook for 5 minutes, or until lightly browned, turning once. Remove from the skillet.
3. Add onion, potatoes, ham, slaw mix and caraway seed to the skillet. Mix well, then top with chicken. Cover and cook for 10-15 minutes, or until vegetables are tender and chicken is done (internal temperature 170°F). Makes 4 servings.

Tips: Serve with hot rye rolls. Refrigerate leftovers.

Variation: Boneless, skinless chicken thigh cutlets can be substituted for the breasts.

* Brands may vary by region; substitute a similar product.

Chicken Monterey
HEINZ ▲

1 15-ounce can black beans
1 tablespoon vegetable oil
1 pound skinless, boneless chicken breast halves
1/2 teaspoon chili powder
1 11-ounce can whole kernel corn, drained
1/2 cup Heinz* Tomato Ketchup
1 large tomato, chopped

1. Drain beans, reserving 1/2 cup liquid; set beans and liquid aside.
2. Heat oil in a large saucepan over medium heat. Add chicken and cook until lightly browned.
3. Stir in chili powder.
4. Add reserved beans and liquid, corn and ketchup. Simmer, covered, for 5-7 minutes, stirring occasionally.
5. Top each serving with chopped tomato. Makes 4 servings.

* Brands may vary by region; substitute a similar product.

Grand Parisian Salad with Garlic Chicken
READY PAC ▲

6 garlic cloves, minced
1/4 cup white vinegar
2 tablespoons dried Italian seasoning
Salt
Freshly cracked pepper
1/2 cup olive oil
4 boneless, skinless chicken breast halves
1 16-ounce bag Ready Pac Grand Parisian Salad

1. Combine garlic, vinegar, Italian seasoning, and salt and pepper to taste in a bowl. Slowly whisk in olive oil until mixed.
2. Poke small holes in the chicken with a fork. Place chicken in a bowl or zipper-lock bag. Add garlic mixture, moving chicken around to coat completely. Cover bowl or seal bag and marinate for at least 30 minutes.
3. Cook chicken on a grill until juices run clear.
4. Place salad ingredients in a bowl and toss. Divide salad among individual plates and top each serving with a sliced chicken breast.
Makes 4 servings.

Chicken Roulade with Bacon
BEAR CREEK ▲

1 package 8-Serve Bear Creek Country Kitchens*
    Creamy Wild Rice Soup Mix
6-8 strips bacon
6-8 boneless, skinless chicken breast halves (pounded flat so
    they can be rolled)
6-8 carrot sticks (3 1/2 by 1/4 by 1/4 inch)
6-8 zucchini sticks (3 1/2 by 1/4 by 1/4 inch)
6-8 sticks of Cheddar, Swiss or mozzarella cheese
    (3 1/2 by 1/2 by 1/2 inch)

1. Preheat oven to 375°F.
2. Prepare soup mix according to package directions, reducing water to 6 1/2 cups.
3. Fry bacon for 1 minute on each side and remove from the pan, saving the drippings.
4. Place chicken in the hot drippings and cook for 2 minutes on each side.
5. Roll 1 carrot stick, 1 zucchini stick and 1 cheese stick in each of the chicken breasts, wrap with bacon and secure with a toothpick.
6. Place chicken in a 9-by-13-inch baking dish and cover with prepared soup. Bake for 45 minutes, or until chicken is cooked through.
Makes 6-8 servings.

Brands may vary by region; substitute a similar product.

Rotisserie Chicken Stir-Fry
KIRKLAND SIGNATURE ▼

¹⁄₄ **cup cornstarch**
2 tablespoons water
1 teaspoon minced fresh ginger
1 teaspoon minced fresh garlic
¹⁄₃ **cup sugar**
¹⁄₄ **cup soy sauce**
2 tablespoons white vinegar
2 tablespoons dry sherry
1 cup canned chicken broth
2 ¹⁄₂ cups Kirkland Signature Stir Fry Vegetables (frozen)
¹⁄₂ **Kirkland Signature Rotisserie Chicken**

1. Combine cornstarch, water, ginger, garlic, sugar, soy sauce, vinegar, sherry and chicken broth in a bowl and stir, or place in a closed container and shake.

2. Heat a large skillet or wok over medium heat. Add vegetables and 2 ¹⁄₂ tablespoons water and cook for 4-5 minutes.

3. Cut chicken meat into bite-size pieces and add to the vegetables. Cook for 3-4 minutes.

4. Add sauce and cook until it thickens. Serve over rice or noodles, if desired. Makes 2-3 servings.

Tips: Use lite soy sauce and reduced-sodium chicken broth for a low-salt version. Add grated orange peel, pineapple juice or orange juice to boost flavor.

KIRKLAND *Signature*

Chicken with Mangoes
PROFOOD ▲

9 ounces Philippine Brand*
  dried mangoes, halved

1 cup flour

1/2 teaspoon salt

1/4 teaspoon baking powder

6 skinless, boneless chicken
  breast halves, cut in
  1/4-inch-wide strips

3 cups vegetable oil

1 thin slice fresh ginger

1 red bell pepper, sliced

1 green bell pepper, sliced

3 tablespoons white vinegar

3 tablespoons dry sherry

4 teaspoons soy sauce

2 teaspoons sugar

2 teaspoons cornstarch

2 teaspoons chicken bouillon

1 teaspoon Asian sesame oil

1 green onion, cut into 8 pieces

1. Soak mangoes in 4 cups lukewarm water for 1 1/2 hours; drain.

2. Combine flour, 1 cup water, salt and baking powder; let stand
for 15 minutes. Stir in chicken.

3. Heat oil in a wok to boiling (375°F). Fry chicken strips until
golden brown.

4. Pour off all but 1 tablespoon oil. Stir-fry ginger over medium heat
until lightly browned. Add peppers.

5. Combine 3/4 cup water, vinegar, sherry, soy sauce, sugar, cornstarch,
bouillon and sesame oil. Add to wok and cook, stirring, until it boils.
Add green onion and simmer for 3 minutes. Add chicken and mangoes;
cook, stirring, for 2 minutes. Makes 4 servings.

*Brands may vary by region; substitute a similar product.

Mesquite-Grilled Chicken
and Artichoke Pizza
KIRKLAND SIGNATURE ▲

3 Roma tomatoes, thinly sliced

1 Kirkland Signature Take-and-Bake 17-inch cheese pizza

2 cups marinated artichoke hearts, drained and rinsed

2-3 frozen boneless mesquite-grilled chicken breasts, thawed, cut in
  1/2-inch cubes

1 medium red onion, thinly sliced

1/3 cup shredded Italian Asiago cheese

1 tablespoon grated Parmesan cheese

1 teaspoon dried oregano

1 teaspoon garlic powder

1 teaspoon chopped fresh parsley

1. Preheat oven to 375°F.

2. Arrange tomato slices evenly over entire pizza. Add artichokes and
cubed chicken. Cover with red onion rings and top with shredded Asiago.

3. Combine Parmesan, oregano and garlic powder in a small bowl.
Sprinkle over the pizza. Garnish with chopped parsley.

4. Place pizza directly on the center oven rack and bake for 12-15
minutes, or until the cheese is completely melted and the crust is a
light golden brown. Remove pizza from the oven and let sit for
3 minutes before cutting and serving. Makes 4-6 servings.

goglanian
BAKERIES, INC.

Crabmeat-Stuffed Mushrooms with Chicken Pot Pie
AMERICA'S KITCHEN ▲

12 silver-dollar-sized mushroom caps, stems removed

1 cup dry white wine

8 ounces cream cheese, softened

2 tablespoons grated Parmesan cheese, plus more for topping

2 teaspoons sherry

1 tablespoon finely diced green onion

1 teaspoon Worcestershire sauce

1 teaspoon hot pepper sauce

1/2 teaspoon ground black pepper

1 tablespoon chopped fresh parsley

1 teaspoon fresh lemon juice

4 ounces lump crabmeat

America's Kitchen Chicken Pot Pie, prepared according to package directions

1. Preheat oven to 400°F.

2. Place mushrooms and wine in a 9-inch sauté pan and cook over medium-high heat for 5-7 minutes, or until mushrooms turn a medium brown. Remove mushrooms and carefully press out excess moisture between paper towels. Cool.

3. In a large bowl, combine cream cheese, 2 tablespoons grated Parmesan, sherry, onion, seasonings and lemon juice; mix well. Gently fold in crab.

4. Stuff mushrooms and top with grated Parmesan. Place on a sheet pan.

5. Bake on the middle oven rack for 20-25 minutes, or until golden and bubbling.

6. Let cool slightly and serve with chicken pot pie. Makes 8-12 servings.

AMERICA'S KITCHEN

Country Garden Alfredo
MRS. DASH AND MOLLY McBUTTER ▲

12 ounces egg noodles

1 16-ounce package frozen mixed vegetables

1 cup 2% milk

1 8-ounce package reduced-fat cream cheese, cubed and softened

3 tablespoons Molly McButter Natural Butter Flavor Sprinkles*

2 teaspoons Mrs. Dash Garlic & Herb Seasoning Blend *or* 2 tablespoons Mrs. Dash Original Blend*

1/2 cup sliced green onions

1. Cook noodles according to package directions.

2. In the last 4 minutes of cooking time, add frozen vegetables to boiling noodles. Drain noodles/vegetable mix; set aside and keep warm.

3. In a separate saucepan, combine milk, cream cheese, Molly McButter and Mrs. Dash. Heat on medium-low until cream cheese is thoroughly melted.

4. Combine hot noodles and vegetables with green onions and sauce, tossing to coat. Makes 6 servings.

* Brands may vary by region; substitute a similar product.

Stuffed Bell Peppers
NEW YORK STYLE SAUSAGE ◄

$^1/_4$ cup *each* white, brown and wild rice
6 medium bell peppers: 2 yellow, 2 red, 2 green
1 pound mild, hot or turkey Italian New York Style Sausage*
1 small onion, chopped
4 garlic cloves, crushed
$^1/_2$ pound fresh small mushrooms, chopped
$^1/_3$ cup finely chopped fresh parsley
$^1/_2$ cup chopped walnuts
$^1/_2$ cup grated Romano cheese
$^1/_4$ teaspoon salt
$^1/_4$ teaspoon ground black pepper
$^1/_2$ teaspoon dried oregano
$^1/_2$ teaspoon dried basil
2 eggs, beaten
Olive oil

1. Prepare rices and set aside.
2. Preheat oven to 350°F.
3. Wash and clean bell peppers. Slice off the tops (approx. $^1/_2$ inch) and clean insides thoroughly.
4. Remove sausage from casing and sauté in a large frying pan over medium heat until crumbled and lightly browned. Using a slotted spoon, transfer sausage to a bowl and set aside.
5. Sauté onion, garlic, mushrooms and parsley in remaining drippings until soft. Add walnuts and sauté for 2 minutes.
6. Add vegetable mixture and cheese to sausage. Stir together and add cooked rice. Add salt, pepper, oregano, basil and beaten eggs. Combine well.
7. Stuff bell peppers with the sausage mixture. Rub the exterior of the peppers with olive oil, place in a baking pan, cover loosely with foil, and bake for 1-1 $^1/_2$ hours, or until peppers are tender. Makes 6 servings.
Tip: Serve peppers "New York Style" by adding sautéed onions, garlic and cooked sausage to your favorite prepared sauce.

* Brands may vary by region; substitute a similar product.

Italian Grana Padano Parmesan
Easy Primavera Pasta Pie
CELLO ▲

CRUST
4 ounces spaghetti
1 egg, beaten
$^1/_3$ cup grated Cello Italian Grana Padano Parmesan
1 tablespoon butter, softened

FILLING
2 tablespoons butter
2 cups broccoli florets
1 small red or green bell pepper, cut in strips
1 medium onion, sliced

2 cups chopped cooked chicken or turkey
$^1/_4$ cup grated Cello Italian Grana Padano Parmesan
$^3/_4$ teaspoon dried Italian seasoning
$^1/_4$ teaspoon salt

TOPPING
2 eggs, beaten
$^1/_2$ cup heavy cream
2 tablespoons grated Cello Italian Grana Padano Parmesan

1. To prepare crust, cook pasta according to package directions; drain. Combine egg, Grana Padano Parmesan and butter. Stir into spaghetti. Press onto bottom and sides of a greased 9-inch pie plate.
2. Preheat oven to 350°F.
3. To prepare filling, melt butter in a large sauté pan over medium heat. Add broccoli, bell pepper and onion; cook until crisp-tender. Add remaining ingredients. Spoon over crust.
4. To prepare topping, combine eggs and cream thoroughly. Pour over vegetables.
5. Cover and bake for 25 minutes. Uncover, sprinkle with 2 tablespoons Grana Padano Parmesan, and bake for 10 minutes, or until browned. Let stand for 10 minutes. Makes 6 servings.

arthur schuman inc.

Entrées

Hot or Sweet Italian Sausage and Bell Pepper Soft Tacos
PREMIO ▾

8 links Premio* Hot or Sweet Italian Sausage, cut into $^1/_2$-inch pieces

1 $^1/_2$ teaspoons dried Italian seasoning

4 tablespoons vegetable oil, divided

4 cups sliced red, yellow and green bell peppers
     (about 4-5 medium peppers)

1 tablespoon or less finely chopped garlic

$^1/_2$ teaspoon salt

Freshly ground black pepper

6-8 soft flour tortillas

1 cup shredded Cheddar or Monterey Jack cheese

1 cup prepared salsa

1. Combine sausage and Italian seasoning. Heat 2 tablespoons oil in a heavy skillet over medium heat and cook sausage for 10-12 minutes, or until no longer pink. Remove from the heat and cover.

2. Sauté peppers and garlic in 2 tablespoons oil over medium heat until tender. Season with salt and pepper to taste.

3. Fill tortillas with sausage, peppers, cheese and salsa. Fold and serve. Makes 6-8 servings.

* Brands may vary by region; substitute a similar product.

Baked Ravioli (Lasagna-Style)
KIRKLAND SIGNATURE/SEVIROLI FOODS ▲

2 tablespoons cooking oil
1 29-ounce can tomato sauce
24 pieces Kirkland Signature Four-Cheese Ravioli
1 ounce grated Romano cheese
14 ounces Kirkland Signature Meatballs, thawed and finely chopped
5 ounces shredded mozzarella cheese

1. Preheat oven to 400°F.
2. Oil an 8-by-10-inch baking pan and spread with 5 ounces of tomato sauce.
3. Place a layer of 12 ravioli, flat side up, on the sauce. Spread 12 ounces of tomato sauce over the ravioli, and cover with half the Romano cheese, half the meatballs and 2 ounces of shredded mozzarella. Pat down lightly.
4. Repeat this procedure, saving 1 ounce of mozzarella for the top. Pat down again and cover with tented aluminum foil.
5. Bake for 1 hour, or until heated through and mozzarella on top is melted. If frozen, bake for an additional 15 minutes. Makes 6-10 servings.

Angel Hair Pasta with Splendido Tomato Chicken Cream Sauce
SUNSET ▲

1 tablespoon olive oil
2 skinless, boneless chicken breast halves, cut into 1-inch cubes
2 garlic cloves, minced
4 tablespoons butter
2 pounds Sunset Splendido* tomatoes: 1 1/2 pounds pureed in blender and 1/2 pound cut in half
1/2 teaspoon salt
1/2 teaspoon freshly ground pepper
12 ounces angel hair pasta
3/4 cup half-and-half
2 tablespoons chopped fresh basil
1/4 cup grated Parmesan cheese

1. Heat olive oil in a skillet over medium heat; add chicken and half of garlic. Cook, stirring, until chicken is cooked through. Remove from skillet.
2. In a separate skillet, heat butter over medium heat. Add remaining garlic and cook, stirring, for 1 minute. Add pureed tomatoes, salt and pepper. Cook until sauce is thickened.
3. Meanwhile, cook pasta according to package directions.
4. Add half-and-half and basil to skillet. Add chicken and 1/2 pound halved tomatoes. Cook for 2 minutes.
5. Pour sauce over pasta and serve, garnished with Parmesan. Makes 4 servings.

Brands may vary by region; substitute a similar product.

Entrées I

Eggplant Gratin
BELGIOIOSO ▼

3 tablespoons corn oil
1 large eggplant, cut into ¹/₂-inch cubes
1 tablespoon butter
¹/₄ cup chopped onion
1 28-ounce can Italian tomatoes, chopped
1 tablespoon chopped fresh basil
¹/₂ cup BelGioioso Ricotta con Latte cheese
1 tablespoon milk
¹/₂ cup plus 2 tablespoons grated BelGioioso Parmesan cheese
1 egg
8 ounces BelGioioso Sliced Mild Provolone cheese

1. Preheat oven to 300°F.

2. Heat oil in a sauté pan over medium-high heat and cook cubed eggplant until lightly browned; set aside.

3. Melt butter over medium heat and sauté onion until soft. Add chopped tomatoes and basil and simmer for 20-30 minutes.

4. While tomatoes are simmering, place ricotta, milk, ¹/₂ cup grated Parmesan and egg in a bowl and mix thoroughly.

5. Layer a greased 9-by-9-inch square baking dish with half of the eggplant, a third of the tomato sauce, half of the ricotta mixture and half of the sliced provolone. Repeat with a second layer. Top with remaining tomato sauce and sprinkle with 2 tablespoons grated Parmesan.

6. Bake for 10-15 minutes, or until cheese is melted and dish is heated through. Makes 4-6 servings.

BELGIOIOSO®
(bel-joy-oso)

Crispy Fried Spinach Cheese Ravioli with Pesto Sauce
CIBO NATURALS/ MONTEREY GOURMET FOODS ▼

¼ cup canola oil
¼ cup (½ stick) butter or margarine
1 36-ounce package fresh Monterey Pasta Spinach & Cheese Ravioli
1 22-ounce jar Kirkland Signature by Cibo Naturals Pesto Sauce
¼ cup grated Parmesan cheese (optional)
⅛ teaspoon salt (optional)
Pinch of ground black pepper or red pepper flakes (optional)

1. Add a portion of the oil and butter to a large (12-inch) skillet and heat over medium heat.
2. When the butter begins to foam, add about ¼ of the ravioli. Sauté on one side for 2 minutes, or until they are golden brown and begin to develop bubbles on the surface. The heat should not be above a medium range, so as to brown the ravioli but not burn.
3. When the first side is browned, turn the ravioli over. When they are golden brown, remove from the pan and place on a dry paper towel to absorb excess oil.
4. Repeat the above process until you've cooked enough ravioli to meet your needs.
5. Place ravioli on a platter and drizzle with pesto sauce or serve sauce in a bowl for dipping.
6. For extra flavor, combine grated Parmesan, salt and pepper. Lightly toss ravioli in the mixture before serving. Makes 10 servings.

Festive Field Greens
JENNIE-O TURKEY STORE ▲

1 cup pecan pieces
$^1/_2$ cup maple syrup
5 ounces baby field greens
$^1/_2$ pound Jennie-O Turkey Store VIP turkey breast, sliced into
 $^1/_4$-inch strips
4 ounces sweetened dried cranberries

VINAIGRETTE
2 tablespoons Dijon mustard
2 tablespoons white wine vinegar or sherry vinegar
2 tablespoons honey
Juice of 1 lemon
Salt and pepper to taste
$^1/_4$ cup olive oil

1. Preheat oven to 350°F.
2. In a small mixing bowl, toss pecans with maple syrup to coat. Spread onto a lightly oiled cookie sheet. Bake for 15-18 minutes, turning with a spatula every 5 minutes. When pecans are toasted, place on a lightly oiled plate and let cool.
3. Meanwhile, prepare the vinaigrette by whisking all the ingredients together.
4. Place salad greens on plates and top with turkey strips. Sprinkle with cranberries and pecans. Drizzle with vinaigrette just before serving. Makes 6 servings.

Chicken 'n Cheese Chimichangas with Grilled Vegetables
EL MONTEREY ▲

4 El Monterey Chicken 'n Cheese Chimichangas
2 zucchini, halved lengthwise
2 yellow summer squash, halved lengthwise
1 green bell pepper, cut into 4 flat sides
1 red bell pepper, cut into 4 flat sides
1 yellow bell pepper, cut into 4 flat sides
12 asparagus spears
4 portobello mushrooms
2 tomatoes, halved
2 white onions, cut in thick horizontal slices
1 cup prepared balsamic vinaigrette
1 $^1/_2$ cups prepared Alfredo sauce
1 $^1/_2$ cups prepared salsa

1. Prepare chimichangas according to package directions.
2. Marinate vegetables in vinaigrette and then grill.
3. Combine Alfredo sauce and salsa in a saucepan; bring to a simmer.
4. Arrange grilled vegetables and chimichangas on a platter. Top with some of the sauce and serve the remainder on the side. Makes 4 servings.

Asparagus Enchiladas
L&M ▼

12 corn tortillas
Cooking spray
1/4 cup margarine
1/3 cup cornstarch or flour
1 1/2 cups chicken broth
1/2 cup fat-free sour cream
1/2 cup red or green taco sauce
1 4 1/2-ounce can diced green chilies, drained
1/2 cup sliced mushrooms
2 1/2 cups shredded cooked chicken
1/2-1 cup diced onion
2 pounds blanched, drained L&M* fresh asparagus, cut into
    1/2-inch pieces
Grated Monterey Jack cheese
Grated Parmesan cheese

1. Preheat oven to 350°F.
2. Spray a sauté pan and tortillas with cooking spray. Heat each tortilla briefly over medium-high heat, roll up and set aside.
3. Add margarine to pan and melt over medium-low heat. Blend in cornstarch. Add broth and cook until thickened. Add sour cream, taco sauce, chilies and mushrooms. Cook until heated through.
4. Mix together chicken, onion and asparagus. Divide among tortillas. Sprinkle with Monterey Jack. Top each with 3 tablespoons sauce and roll up.
5. Place side by side in a 9-by-13-inch pan. Top with remaining sauce, Monterey Jack and Parmesan.
6. Bake for 25 minutes, or until heated through. Makes 6 servings.

Brands may vary by region; substitute a similar product.

Creamy Cranberry Vinaigrette Salad
POCKET MEALS ▲

1/3 cup cranberry juice
3 tablespoons balsamic vinegar
2 tablespoons Dijon mustard
1 teaspoon crushed garlic
1 tablespoon plain yogurt
1/2 cup olive oil
Salt and pepper
Salad greens

1. Combine cranberry juice, vinegar, mustard and garlic in a food processor
or blender.
2. Whisk yogurt into blended ingredients.
3. Whisk olive oil into blended ingredients.
4. Add salt and pepper to taste.
5. Toss vinaigrette with your favorite salad greens. Refrigerate any
unused vinaigrette. Makes 6-8 servings.

Tip: Serve with Pocket Meals by Hot Pockets* Pepperoni Pizza, or Bistro's
by Hot Pockets* Sausage, Pepperoni and Cheese Stuffed Sandwiches.

Brands may vary by region; substitute a similar product.

Louisiana Hot Sausage Jambalaya
EVERGOOD FINE FOODS ▲

1 stick (4 ounces) butter
2 red onions, chopped
4 celery ribs, diced
1 green bell pepper, chopped
4 green onions, chopped
3 garlic cloves, finely chopped
2 bay leaves
1 jalapeño pepper, finely chopped
1 tablespoon Creole seasoning
1/4 teaspoon cayenne pepper

1/2 teaspoon fresh thyme
1 28-ounce can whole tomatoes
1 pound Evergood* Louisiana Hot
   Link Sausage, cut into
   1/2-inch pieces
1/2 pound jumbo shrimp
3/4 pound smoked ham, cut into
   1/2-inch pieces
2 14 1/2-ounce cans chicken broth
3 cups long-grain rice

1. Melt butter in a large Dutch oven over medium-high heat.
2. Add all fresh vegetables and seasoning ingredients. Cover and cook
for about 15 minutes.
3. Add whole tomatoes, sausage, shrimp, ham, broth and rice.
4. Bring to a simmer, reduce heat to low, cover and cook, stirring
occasionally, for 1 hour, or until the rice is tender. Makes 10 servings.

Brands may vary by region; substitute a similar product.

Franks with Roasted Corn Relish
HEBREW NATIONAL ▲

1 ¹/₂ cups frozen whole-kernel corn
3 green onions, thinly sliced
1 tablespoon finely chopped red bell pepper
2 tablespoons Italian salad dressing
¹/₄ teaspoon garlic salt
1 12-ounce package Hebrew National Beef Franks (7 franks)
7 hot dog buns

1. Heat a large nonstick skillet over medium-high heat.

2. Add corn and cook, stirring, for 3 minutes, or until corn is lightly browned. Remove from the skillet and place in a medium bowl.

3. Add onions, bell pepper, salad dressing and garlic salt to the bowl and mix well.

4. Grill franks according to package directions. Toast buns.

5. Place franks in buns and top with the corn mixture. Makes 7 servings.

Monster Chili
MONSTER ENERGY ▲

2 tablespoons olive oil
1 cup chopped onion
1 ¹/₄ cups chopped green bell pepper
3 garlic cloves, crushed
1 ¹/₂ pounds boneless chicken breast, cut in cubes
1 14 ¹/₂-ounce can *each* red kidney beans, black beans and pinto beans, well drained
1 14 ¹/₂-ounce can diced tomatoes, drained
1 16-ounce can Monster Energy* Drink
1 4 ¹/₂-ounce can chopped green chilies
¹/₄ cup chicken broth
2 tablespoons chili powder
1 teaspoon ground cumin
1 tablespoon salt
¹/₂ cup grated mozzarella cheese
Cilantro sprigs, for garnish

1. Heat olive oil in a sauté pan over medium heat. Add onion, bell pepper and garlic; cook until onion is translucent. Add chicken and sauté until lightly browned. Transfer to a slow cooker.

2. Add beans, tomatoes, energy drink, chilies, chicken broth, chili powder, cumin and salt. Cover and cook on medium-low for 4-6 hours for monsterous flavor!

3. Serve with grated cheese and garnish with cilantro sprigs. Makes 6-plus monster portions.

* Brands may vary by region; substitute a similar product.

Entrées

BBQ Burgers in Lettuce Wraps
TANIMURA & ANTLE/DENICE & FILICE ▲

1 ¹/₂ Denice & Filice* Italian sweet red onions
2 teaspoons balsamic vinegar
2 teaspoons extra-virgin olive oil
Salt
4 ground beef patties, ¹/₃ pound each
4 slices Monterey Jack cheese
4 large leaves and 4 medium leaves Tanimura & Antle* iceberg lettuce
²/₃ cup of your favorite barbecue dressing

1. Peel onions and cut into four ¹/₂-inch-thick horizontal slices. Drizzle each slice with ¹/₂ teaspoon balsamic vinegar and ¹/₂ teaspoon olive oil; season to taste with salt.
2. Grill or pan-fry burgers and onions for about 3 minutes per side, or until cooked to taste. Top each burger with 1 slice cheese and cook just until cheese melts.
3. To serve, place each burger on a large lettuce leaf. Add 1 slice onion and barbecue dressing to taste. Top with a smaller lettuce leaf. Bring bottom leaf up and around burger to enclose. Makes 4 servings.

Creative Idea: Substitute large portabello mushrooms for ground beef patties. Omit the barbecue dressing; instead, drizzle top and bottom of mushrooms with balsamic vinegar, olive oil and soy sauce. Grill or pan fry, then top with onion and wrap in lettuce.

Brands may vary by region; substitute a similar product.

Sweet Onion Beef Oscar Napoleon
KEYSTONE ▲

5 tablespoons butter, divided
12 slices white bread, trimmed to 3-by-3-inch squares (or puff pastry)
1 tablespoon olive oil
2 Keystone* Certified Sweet Onions, sliced
16 ounces jumbo lump crabmeat
1 .90-ounce packet béarnaise sauce
4 5-ounce filet mignon steaks
Fresh tarragon, for garnish
Paprika, for garnish

1. Melt 2 tablespoons butter and use to lightly brush both sides of bread slices. Place on a baking sheet and toast under the broiler for 1-2 minutes, or until golden brown on both sides.
2. Heat 2 tablespoons butter and olive oil in a sauté pan over high heat and cook onions for 8-12 minutes, or until lightly caramelized; keep warm.
3. Sauté crabmeat in 1 tablespoon butter; keep warm.
4. Make béarnaise according to packet directions.
5. Grill beef filets to desired doneness; keep warm.
6. Place 1 bread square on each plate. Top with a beef filet, then another square. Add crabmeat and another square. Top with onions. Spoon on béarnaise sauce and garnish with a sprig of tarragon and a sprinkle of paprika on the plate rim. Makes 4 servings.

Recipe courtesy of Chef Dave Munson.
Brands may vary by region; substitute a similar product.

Cheese Burgers
PPCS LIMITED ▲

1 ¹/₂ pounds Kirkland Signature* ground beef
1 cup grated or finely diced Colby or Edam cheese
¹/₂ cup chopped fresh parsley
1 small onion, peeled and finely diced
1 egg
2-3 slices bread, broken into crumbs
¹/₂ cup barbecue sauce
Salt and pepper
Hamburger buns
Sliced beets
Sliced tomatoes
Lettuce

1. In a bowl, combine ground beef, cheese, parsley, onion, egg, bread crumbs, barbecue sauce, and salt and pepper to taste. Mold into 8 evenly shaped patties.

2. Cook over medium heat on a greased barbecue or in a frying pan for 5-7 minutes on each side, or until cooked to taste.

3. Alternatively, broil the burgers under medium-high heat for the same amount of time until cooked and golden.

4. Serve the burgers on crispy buns with sliced beets, sliced tomato and lettuce, accompanied by your favorite potato salad. Makes 8 servings.

Recipe courtesy of Allyson Gofton, Hot Ideas for Beef and Lamb.
* Brands may vary by region; substitute a similar product.

Kung Pao Tuna
CHICKEN OF THE SEA ▲

1 tablespoon soy sauce
2 tablespoons seasoned rice vinegar
1 tablespoon sake (Japanese rice wine)
¹/₂-1 teaspoon red pepper flakes
1 tablespoon chopped unsalted peanuts
1 tablespoon chopped green bell pepper
1 tablespoon chopped red bell pepper
1 ¹/₂ tablespoons chopped green onion
2 6-ounce cans Chicken of the Sea Chunk Light Tuna in water or Albacore Tuna in water, drained
4 lettuce leaves, washed and patted dry (optional)

1. In a bowl, whisk together soy sauce, vinegar, sake and red pepper flakes until well blended.

2. Stir in peanuts, bell pepper and onion.

3. Gently flake and fold in tuna; mix until ingredients are blended.

4. Chill until ready to serve. If desired, serve in lettuce cups.
Makes 4 servings.

Entrées I

Chicago-Style English Muffin Club
GEORGE WESTON BAKERIES

1 Thomas' English Muffin
2 pieces romaine lettuce
1 3- to 4-ounce boneless, skinless chicken breast, grilled
2 thin slices tomato
1 ounce ham, thinly sliced
2 thin slices Swiss cheese
2 slices bacon, cooked and drained
2 rings green bell pepper
1/4 cup Thousand Island dressing
1 hard-boiled egg, sliced

1. Split English muffin in half and toast. Place on a serving plate. Cover with lettuce.

2. Slice chicken horizontally into 4 pieces.

3. Layer chicken, tomato, ham, Swiss cheese, bacon, and bell pepper on English muffin halves.

4. Spoon dressing overall. Top with sliced egg. Serve immediately. Makes 1 serving.

Weston
George Weston Bakeries Inc.

Ham and Avocado Torta
LA BREA BAKERY ▲

¹/₂ slightly soft avocado
1 tablespoon mayonnaise
1 La Brea Bakery ciabatta roll, sliced in half
4 ounces ham, about 5 thin slices
3 ounces queso fresco, sliced ¹/₃- to ¹/₂-inch thick
2 ounces jalapeño pepper, seeded and chopped

1. Scoop out the avocado flesh and place in a bowl; mash coarsely with a fork. Blend in mayonnaise to make a chunky spread.

2. Spread avocado mayonnaise thickly on both sides of the ciabatta roll. Fold ham in twists and place on the bottom of the roll. Place queso fresco slices on the ham. Top with a generous amount of jalapeños. Makes 1 serving.

Chicken, Pesto and Pepper Sandwiches
CAMPBELL'S ▲

¹/₂ cup prepared pesto sauce
4 Pepperidge Farm* Sandwich Buns
4 boneless chicken breast halves
4 slices mozzarella cheese
Lettuce
1 7-ounce jar roasted red peppers, drained
Campbell's* Select Gold Label Italian Tomato Soup

1. Spread about 1 teaspoon pesto sauce on each bun half.

2. Grill or broil chicken for 15 minutes, or until done, turning and brushing with remaining pesto sauce during the last 5 minutes of cooking time.

3. Top chicken breasts with cheese.

4. Layer bottom bun halves with lettuce, chicken and roasted red peppers, then top with remaining bun halves.

5. Serve with Select Gold Label Italian Tomato Soup. Makes 4 servings.

Brands may vary by region; substitute a similar product.

Desserts

Cherry Compote
GROWER DIRECT/
WESTERN SWEET CHERRY ◀

1 cup pomegranate juice

1 cup dried tart cherries

1 1/2 pounds fresh sweet Western Sweet* cherries, halved and pitted, or 20 ounces frozen pitted Bing cherries, halved

1/2 cup sugar

1 tablespoon brandy

1 tablespoon rum

2 teaspoons cornstarch

Orange zest (optional)

1. Place pomegranate juice and dried cherries in a large heavy saucepan and bring to a boil. Remove from the heat, cover and let steep for 20 minutes.

2. Bring dried cherry mixture to a simmer. Stir in fresh or frozen cherries and sugar. Simmer until cherries soften, about 2 minutes for fresh and 5 minutes for frozen.

3. In a small bowl, mix brandy and rum; blend in cornstarch. Slowly stir into cherries. Cook over medium heat until the mixture boils and thickens, about 1 minute.

4. Let cool, then cover and refrigerate until cold. Garnish with orange zest, if desired. Makes 8 servings.

* Brands may vary by region; substitute a similar product.

California Peach Crisp
SunWest ▲

3 pounds ripe fresh SunWest* California peaches

1 cup sugar

1/2 cup all-purpose flour

1/2 cup granola (no dried fruit)

1/2 teaspoon freshly grated nutmeg

1/8 teaspoon salt

1/2 stick (1/4 cup) unsalted butter, softened

1/4 cup fresh orange juice

1. Preheat oven to 375°F.

2. Cut an X on blossom end of peaches and place in boiling water for 10 seconds. Peel and cut into 3/4-inch slices.

3. In a bowl, stir together sugar, flour, granola, nutmeg and salt. Work in butter with a pastry blender or your fingertips until small clumps form.

4. Spread peaches in a lightly buttered 9-by-13-inch baking dish. Toss peaches with orange juice. Top with crumb mixture.

5. Bake on the middle oven rack until topping is golden and peaches are tender, 35-40 minutes. Cool slightly and serve warm. Makes 6 servings.

* Brands may vary by region; substitute a similar product.

Delicious Clementines
ACONEX ▼

12 regular-sized Aconex clementines
1 ¹/₂ cups sugar
¹/₂ cup clementine juice
¹/₂ cup water
¹/₂ cup of your preferred liquor (cognac or rum), warmed

1. With a vegetable peeler, completely remove the peel from the clementines, trimming off any bitter white pith. Place in a saucepan with sugar, clementine juice and water. Bring to a boil and cook, stirring, until the sugar has dissolved and a light syrup forms. Remove from the heat and let cool. Strain.

2. Remove remaining peel from clementines and section the fruit. Place the fruit sections in a saucepan. Heat the syrup until almost boiling and pour over the clementines.

3. Immediately add warmed liquor to the pan and ignite with a match. When the flame has died down, serve the clementines and syrup.
Makes 6 servings.

Tip: Serve with cream or vanilla ice cream.

◼️ACONEX 🍐

Florida Ambrosia
DNE WORLD FRUIT ▲

¹/₄ cup sugar

1 tablespoon cornstarch

1 teaspoon finely shredded Florida orange peel

1 cup Florida orange juice

2 teaspoons fresh lemon juice

3 Florida oranges, peeled, sliced and seeded

2 Florida grapefruit, peeled, sectioned and seeded

1 cup halved seedless green and/or red grapes

6 angel-cake wedges or meringue shells

1. In a small saucepan, stir together sugar and cornstarch. Stir in orange peel and orange juice. Cook, stirring, over medium heat until thickened and bubbly. Continue cooking and stirring for 2 minutes more. Remove sauce from heat; stir in lemon juice. Cover and let cool.

2. Meanwhile, combine oranges, grapefruit and grapes in a 1 ¹/₂-quart bowl. Pour orange sauce over fruit and stir. Cover and chill for up to 6 hours.

3. To serve, spoon fruit mixture over cake wedges or into meringue shells. Makes 6 servings.

Asian Pears with Gingered Pluot Sauce
KINGSBURG ORCHARDS ▲

6 Dinosaur Brand pluots, pitted

2 teaspoons lemon juice

¹/₄ cup water

¹/₂ cup packed dark brown sugar

¹/₄ teaspoon ground ginger

4 large Kingsburg Orchards Asian pears, chilled

¹/₄ cup toasted chopped walnuts or pecans

Whipped cream or crème fraîche

1. Puree pluots in a food processor.

2. Combine lemon juice, water and brown sugar in a saucepan. Add pluot puree and cook mixture on medium heat for 10 minutes, stirring constantly. Add ginger and cook for 2 minutes. Let cool slightly.

3. Slice pears into ¹/₄-inch wedges and arrange slices in a pinwheel pattern on 6 dessert plates. Spoon sauce over pears and top with toasted nuts and a dollop of whipped cream or crème fraîche. Makes 6 servings.

Desserts I

Baked Apples with Hazelnut and Orange
DOMEX ▼

4 Washington baking apples, such as Fuji or Braeburn
¾ cup orange juice, preferably fresh squeezed
½ cup finely chopped toasted hazelnuts
¼ cup packed dark brown sugar
1 ½ teaspoons grated orange peel
¼ teaspoon ground cinnamon
4 teaspoons Frangelico or brandy (optional)
2 tablespoons unsalted butter, cut into 4 pieces

1. Preheat oven to 375°F.

2. Core apples from the stem end, using a melon-baller or small spoon; be careful not to break through the bottom of the apple. Drizzle a little of the orange juice into each apple core to prevent browning.

3. Set apples upright in an 8- or 9-inch square baking dish, preferably so that the apples aren't touching.

4. Combine hazelnuts, brown sugar, grated orange peel and cinnamon in a medium bowl and stir to evenly mix. Spoon the mixture into the apples, pressing lightly as you go.

5. Add 1 teaspoon of Frangelico to each apple and top the filling with a piece of butter. Pour orange juice into the baking dish around the apples.

6. Bake until the apples are tender when pierced with the tip of a knife, 1-1 ¼ hours. Set the pan on a wire rack to cool for 10-15 minutes before serving.

7. Transfer the apples to individual serving plates, drizzle with baking juices and serve. Makes 4 servings.

Tips: Walnuts can be used instead of hazelnuts. Vanilla ice cream is an ideal accompaniment, drizzled with some of the flavorful baking juices.

Recipe created by Cynthia Nims.

Double Berry Crumble
GLOBAL BERRY FARMS ▲

7 cups Naturipe* strawberries, cleaned and quartered
3 cups Naturipe* blueberries, rinsed and drained
1 1/2 cups plus 1 tablespoon flour, divided
1/2 cup plus 1 tablespoon packed light brown sugar, divided
3/4 cup butter
1 teaspoon ground cinnamon
1 teaspoon ground ginger

1. Preheat oven to 375°F.
2. Place berries in a bowl and toss gently with 1 tablespoon flour and
1 tablespoon brown sugar. Pour berries into a buttered 9-by-13-inch
glass baking dish.
3. Combine 1 1/2 cups flour and butter in a bowl and blend together with
a fork until crumbly. Stir in 1/2 cup brown sugar, cinnamon and ginger.
4. Spoon flour mixture evenly over berry mixture.
5. Bake until bubbly, not more than 30 minutes. Makes 10-12 servings.

Tip: Spoon into footed bowls and garnish with fresh strawberries, fresh
mint leaves and whipped cream.

* Brands may vary by region; substitute a similar product.

Baked Apples with Granola
SAGE FRUIT COMPANY ▲

1 1/2 cups low-fat granola
1/3 cup raisins
1 teaspoon ground cinnamon
1/4 cup pure maple syrup
6 medium to large Sage Fruit* Granny Smith apples
3 tablespoons unsalted butter
1 cup apple cider
8 ounces vanilla yogurt
1 tablespoon honey

1. Preheat oven to 350°F.
2. Place granola, raisins, cinnamon and maple syrup in a small mixing
bowl and combine well.
3. Scoop out the core from the top of each apple. Cut a small slice off the
bottom so that it sits flat, but do not cut into the core opening.
4. Stuff each apple with 1/4 cup of the granola mixture and dot with
1/2 tablespoon butter. Place in a shallow baking dish and pour apple cider
around the apples. Bake the apples, basting occasionally, for about 1 hour,
or until fork-tender and caramelized.
5. Mix together yogurt and honey; drizzle over or serve with baked
apples. Makes 6 servings.

* Brands may vary by region; substitute a similar product.

Desserts I

Apple Strudel
CHELAN FRESH ▼

3 large Chelan Fresh* cooking apples (Granny Smith or Fuji),
    peeled and thinly sliced
1/2 cup granulated sugar
1/2 cup raisins
1/2 cup chopped walnuts
1/2 teaspoon ground cinnamon
1/4 teaspoon grated nutmeg
1/4 teaspoon salt
3/4 cup dried bread crumbs, divided
1/2 pound prepared phyllo dough
1/2 cup butter, melted
Confectioners' sugar

1. Preheat oven to 375°F. Grease a large cookie sheet.
2. In a large bowl, toss apples with granulated sugar, raisins, walnuts, cinnamon, nutmeg, salt and 1/4 cup bread crumbs.

3. Cut two 24-inch lengths of waxed paper; overlap two lengthwise sides about 2 inches; fasten with tape. On the waxed paper, overlap a few sheets of phyllo to make a 12-by-16-inch rectangle, brushing sheets where they overlap with some melted butter. Brush the entire rectangle with melted butter and sprinkle with a scant tablespoon of bread crumbs. Repeat, brushing each layer with butter and sprinkling every other layer with crumbs.
4. Starting along one long side of phyllo, spoon apple mixture to cover about 1/2 of the rectangle. From the apple mixture side, roll up jelly-roll fashion. Place on the cookie sheet, seam side down. Brush with melted butter.
5. Bake for 40 minutes, or until golden. Cool on the cookie sheet for 30 minutes.
6. To serve, sprinkle strudel with confectioners' sugar; slice. Serve warm or cold. Makes 14 servings.

* Brands may vary by region; substitute a similar product.

"Good for You" Apple Crisp
NEW YORK APPLE/PENNSYLVANIA APPLE ▲

3/4 cup oatmeal

1/4 cup flour

1/4 cup packed light brown sugar

1/2 teaspoon ground cinnamon

1/2 teaspoon grated nutmeg

2 tablespoons butter or margarine

6 Eastern* apples (Empire, Fuji or Jonagold)

1/4 cup sweetened dried cranberries

1 cup vanilla yogurt

1. Combine oatmeal, flour, sugar and spices in a bowl. Cut in butter or margarine and set aside.

2. Peel and core apples. Slice thin and combine with dried cranberries.

3. Pour apple mixture into an 8-by-8-inch baking dish. Sprinkle with oatmeal mixture.

4. Microwave on high for 12 minutes. Serve hot with vanilla yogurt as a topping. Makes 4 servings.

Brands may vary by region; substitute a similar product.

Apple Dumplings
L&M ▲

Pastry for a 2-crust 9-inch pie

6 medium L&M* Granny Smith apples

SYRUP

2 cups water

1 cup sugar

3 tablespoons butter

1/2 teaspoon ground cinnamon

FILLINGS

Raisins mixed with cinnamon-sugar blend, dotted with butter

or

Dried cranberries mixed with sugar

or

Red-hot candies

1. Preheat oven to 400°F.

2. To prepare syrup, combine all ingredients in a saucepan, bring to a boil and simmer until sugar is dissolved.

3. Roll out pastry to 1/8-inch thickness and cut into six 7-inch squares.

4. Peel and core apples. Place apples on the pastry squares. Fill the cavities with choice of filling. Bring opposite points of pastry up over each apple. Overlap, moisten and seal.

5. Place carefully in a 9-by-12-inch baking dish. Pour hot syrup around dumplings.

6. Bake for 20 minutes, or until golden brown. Makes 6 servings.

Recipe created by Linda Mathews of L&M in Selah, Washington.

Brands may vary by region; substitute a similar product.

Desserts I

Classic Apple Pie
COLUMBIA MARKETING INTERNATIONAL ▼

Pastry dough for 2-crust 9-inch pie
8 medium CMI Granny Smith apples (enough to yield 8 cups sliced)
$1/2$ cup plus 1 tablespoon granulated sugar
$1/4$ cup packed light brown sugar
1 $1/2$ tablespoons fresh lemon juice
1 teaspoon grated lemon peel
$1/4$ teaspoon salt
$1/4$ teaspoon freshly grated nutmeg
$1/4$ teaspoon ground cinnamon
$1/8$ teaspoon ground allspice
1 egg white, lightly beaten

1. Adjust oven rack to center position and preheat oven to 425°F.
2. Roll out half of pastry dough and place in a 9-inch pie pan.

3. Peel, core and cut apples into $1/2$- to $3/4$-inch slices. Place in a bowl and toss with $1/2$ cup granulated sugar, brown sugar, lemon juice, grated lemon peel, salt, nutmeg, cinnamon and allspice. Turn fruit mixture, including juices, into pie shell and mound slightly in center.
4. Roll out remaining dough and place over filling. Trim top and bottom edges to $1/2$ inch beyond pan lip. Tuck this rim of dough underneath itself so that folded edge is flush with pan lip. Flute edging or press with fork tines to seal. Cut four slits at right angles on dough top. Brush crust with egg white and sprinkle evenly with remaining 1 tablespoon sugar.
5. Bake until top crust is golden, about 25 minutes. Reduce heat to 375°F; continue baking until juices bubble and crust is deep golden brown, 30-35 minutes. Transfer pie to a wire rack; cool to almost room temperature, at least 4 hours. Makes 8 servings.

Recipe created by Chef Leslie James.

The "Great Pumpkin" Pumpkin Pie
SPLENDA ▲

1/2 15-ounce package refrigerated piecrust

1 15-ounce can pumpkin

3/4 cup SPLENDA No Calorie Sweetener, Granular

1/3 cup packed dark brown sugar

2 teaspoons ground cinnamon

2 teaspoons ground ginger

1/2 teaspoon salt

1/8 teaspoon ground cloves

3/4 cup half-and-half

3 large eggs, lightly beaten

1 teaspoon vanilla extract

1. Preheat oven to 375°F.

2. Unfold piecrust; press out fold lines. Fit piecrust into a 9-inch pie pan according to package directions; fold edges under and crimp.

3. Stir together pumpkin, SPLENDA No Calorie Sweetener, brown sugar, cinnamon, ginger, salt, cloves and half-and-half until blended. Add eggs and vanilla, stirring until well blended. Pour filling into piecrust.

4. Bake for 50-60 minutes, or until set in the center. Cool completely on a wire rack. Makes 8 servings.

Fruit Pizza
DEL MONTE FRESH PRODUCE ▲

Nonstick cooking spray

1 prepared thin-crust 12-inch pizza crust

8 ounces light cream cheese, softened

1/3 cup sugar

1/2 teaspoon vanilla extract

1 banana, peeled and sliced

4 cups assorted fresh fruit from Del Monte* fruit tray: grapes, mango, pineapple and strawberries

1/4 cup raisins

1/4 cup pecans or pistachios, chopped

1. Preheat oven to 350°F.

2. Spray a 12-inch pizza pan with cooking spray. Place crust on the pan and bake for 8-10 minutes. Cool.

3. In a small bowl, blend cream cheese, sugar and vanilla. Spread mixture over cooled crust.

4. Arrange banana slices in a layer over cream cheese mixture.

5. Arrange remaining fruit slices in circles on bananas, varying colors and shapes.

6. Sprinkle with raisins and nuts.

7. Cut into 10 wedges. Makes 10 servings.

* Brands may vary by region; substitute a similar product.

![Del Monte Quality logo]

Fruit Gold Tart
I.M. RIPE

1 cup crushed graham crackers

2 tablespoons margarine, melted

2 large packages instant vanilla pudding

2-2 1/2 cups milk

1/4 cup thinly sliced dried apricots

2 I.M. RIPE plums, sliced

2 I.M. RIPE nectarines, sliced

2 I.M. RIPE peaches, sliced

3 tablespoons all-fruit jam, melted

1. Preheat oven to 375°F.

2. Mix crumbs with margarine; press into the bottom and slightly up the sides of a 9-inch tart pan with a removable bottom. Bake for 6 minutes, or until crisp. Remove from the oven and let cool.

3. In a medium bowl, combine pudding mix with milk, whisking vigorously to blend. Pour into the tart pan.

4. Sprinkle dried apricots over filling. Arrange sliced fruit on top. Brush fruit with jam to glaze. Chill until ready to serve (best within 4 hours).

5. To serve, gently slip off pan sides. This tart base is delicate, so after cutting, gently slide each wedge onto a dessert plate using a wide metal spatula. Makes 6 servings.

Fresh Fruit Tart
FOWLER PACKING

CRUST

1 1/2 cups flour

2 tablespoons confectioners' sugar

1 1/2 sticks butter, softened

1 egg

FILLING

8 ounces cream cheese, softened

1 cup confectioners' sugar

8 ounces frozen whipped dessert topping, thawed

2 Fowler Packing peaches or nectarines, sliced

1 Fowler Packing plum, sliced

1/2 cup red or green Samsons grapes, sliced

1. Preheat oven to 350°F.

2. To prepare the crust, mix flour and confectioners' sugar in a medium bowl. Cut in butter with a pastry blender. Whisk egg and stir into the dough. Knead to form a ball. Press dough onto the bottom and sides of a 9-inch round fluted tart pan with removable rim. Bake for 12-15 minutes, or until lightly browned. Remove from the oven and cool completely.

3. To make the filling, place cream cheese and confectioners' sugar in a medium bowl and beat well. Fold in whipped topping.

4. Spread filling in the cooled tart shell. Top with fresh fruit. Slice and serve. Makes 8 servings.

Two-Berry Tart with Chocolate Drizzle
GLOBAL BERRY FARMS ▼

1 ready-to-use refrigerated piecrust
1 small box instant lemon pudding (4-serving size)
1 ³/₄ cups milk
1 tablespoon fresh lemon juice
2 cups Naturipe* strawberries, cleaned and sliced
1 cup Naturipe* blueberries, rinsed and drained in a separate bowl
2 tablespoons apricot or apple jelly
¹/₂ cup semisweet chocolate chips

1. Press piecrust into a 10-inch tart pan and bake according to directions. Can be done 1 day ahead.
2. Mix pudding with milk and lemon juice. Pour into cooled piecrust.

3. Arrange sliced strawberries on the tart in a circular pattern, working from outside to inside, overlapping where necessary.
4. Sprinkle blueberries over strawberries.
5. Melt jelly (thin with 1 tablespoon water if necessary) and brush over fruit.
6. Melt chocolate chips and drizzle over fruit. Serve within 4 hours. Refrigerate leftovers. Makes 12 servings.

Tips: Garnish with mint or strawberry leaves. For an easy, even drizzle, place the melted chocolate in a plastic bag, snip the tip and squeeze the chocolate in lines across the top of the tart.

* Brands may vary by region; substitute a similar product.

Easy Mango Sorbet
READY PAC ▲

1 32-ounce package Ready Pac* fresh mango
1 ¹/₂ cups hot water
1 cup sugar
¹/₂ teaspoon lemon juice

1. Place mango in a food processor and puree.
2. Combine water, sugar and lemon juice in a saucepan over low heat. Stir until sugar is dissolved completely. Do not boil.
3. In a bowl, stir together mango puree and sugar mixture. Pour into a freezer-safe plastic bowl or an ice cream maker and put in the freezer for 1 hour, or until the mixture firms and looks fluffy. Makes 6-8 servings.

Brands may vary by region; substitute a similar product.

Stuffed Medjool Dates
SUNDATE ▲

4 ounces cream cheese or mascarpone, softened
1 tablespoon granulated sugar
1 teaspoon vanilla extract
1 tablespoon orange juice
Grated orange peel
16 SunDate* Medjool dates
Ground cinnamon or nutmeg

1. Combine cream cheese, sugar, vanilla, orange juice and grated orange peel to taste. Blend well until smooth.
2. Cut and remove the pits from dates.
3. Spoon or pipe the filling into the dates. Sprinkle with a very light dusting of cinnamon or nutmeg. Makes 4-8 servings.
Variations: Other stuffing options are plain cream cheese, chopped walnuts, almonds or other nuts, and nut butters.

Brands may vary by region; substitute a similar product.

Frozen Grape and Lemon Treats
RICHARD BAGDASARIAN, INC./STEVCO ▼

¹/₂ cup graham cracker crumbs
1 tablespoon honey
1 tablespoon butter or margarine, melted
1 cup California* seedless grapes
1 cup low-fat milk
1 8-ounce container low-fat lemon yogurt
1 3.4-ounce package lemon instant pudding and pie filling mix
1 ¹/₂ cups low-fat whipped dessert topping
Grapes, cut into small wedges, for garnish
12 small California grape clusters, for garnish (optional)

1. Combine graham cracker crumbs, honey and butter; mix well. Line 12 muffin cups with paper cupcake liners; sprinkle 2-3 teaspoons of the crumb mixture in each.
2. Place grapes on top of crumbs.
3. Combine milk and yogurt in a medium bowl. Add pudding/pie mix and blend with a wire whisk for about 1 minute, or until well mixed. Gently stir in whipped topping. Divide among cupcake liners, mounding mixture on top.
4. Freeze for at least 6 hours.
5. Decorate top of dessert with grape wedges in a pinwheel pattern. Garnish with grape clusters, if desired. Makes 12 servings.
* Brands may vary by region; substitute a similar product.

Desserts ▌

Rustic Peach Galette
SUN-MAID RAISINS ▲

1 cup Sun-Maid Natural Raisins
¹/₂ cup granulated sugar
2 tablespoons all-purpose flour
¹/₂ teaspoon ground cinnamon
¹/₄ teaspoon salt
4 cups fresh (or 16 ounces frozen) sliced peaches
1 tablespoon lemon juice
1 9-inch unbaked pie dough round or shell
Powdered sugar

1. Preheat oven to 425°F.

2. Combine raisins, sugar, flour, cinnamon and salt in a bowl.

3. Mix in peaches and lemon juice.

4. Place pie dough on a rimmed baking sheet. Mound fruit in center of dough, leaving a 1- to 2-inch border. Fold dough up, gently pleating and pressing against fruit.

5. Bake for 10 minutes; reduce temperature to 350°F and bake for 20-25 minutes, or until the crust is golden brown. Juices may seep out onto the pan. Remove from the oven and let cool on the pan. With a large spatula, carefully transfer galette to a platter. Dust with powdered sugar just before serving. Makes 8 servings.

Rugala Martini
COUNTRYSIDE BAKING ▲

¹/₄ cup sugar
1 teaspoon cocoa
Martini glass
Lemon slice
¹/₂ cup vanilla ice cream, softened
2 pieces Countryside* Rugala: 1 chocolate and 1 raspberry
¹/₂ cup fresh whipped cream
¹/₄ cup fresh raspberries

1. Mix sugar and cocoa together and place on a saucer.

2. Wipe the rim of the martini glass with the lemon slice and dip in cocoa-sugar mixture to coat rim.

3. Press softened ice cream into the bottom of the martini glass. Place in the freezer for 1 hour.

4. Remove martini glass from the freezer and crumble chocolate rugala over the ice cream. Layer half of whipped cream over crumbled rugala.

5. Crumble raspberry rugala over whipped cream. Layer remaining whipped cream over crumbled rugala.

6. Top with fresh raspberries. Makes 1 serving.

Brands may vary by region; substitute a similar product.

Chocolatey Peanut Butter Bars
JIF ▼

$^1\!/_2$ **Regular Crisco Stick or** $^1\!/_2$ **cup Regular Crisco all-vegetable shortening, plus more for greasing pan**
$^1\!/_2$ **cup granulated sugar**
$^1\!/_2$ **cup firmly packed light brown sugar**
1 egg
1 tablespoon water
$^1\!/_3$ **cup plus 2 tablespoons Jif* Creamy Peanut Butter**
$^1\!/_2$ **teaspoon vanilla extract**
1 cup all-purpose flour
1 cup quick oats (uncooked)
$^1\!/_2$ **teaspoon baking soda**
$^1\!/_4$ **teaspoon salt**
1 cup (6-ounce package) semisweet chocolate chips
$^1\!/_4$ **cup confectioners' sugar**
1-2 teaspoons evaporated milk
Milk chocolate English toffee bits (optional)

1. Preheat oven to 350°F. Grease a 9-by-13-by-2-inch glass baking dish with Crisco.
2. Combine $^1\!/_2$ stick or $^1\!/_2$ cup Crisco shortening, granulated sugar, brown sugar, egg and water in a large bowl. Beat with an electric mixer at medium speed until well blended. Beat in $^1\!/_3$ cup Jif peanut butter and vanilla.
3. In a bowl, combine flour, oats, baking soda and salt. Add gradually to creamed mixture at low speed until well blended. Spread in the baking dish.
4. Bake for 20-25 minutes, or until light brown. Remove pan from the oven and immediately sprinkle chocolate chips over the hot baked cookie base. Let stand for 5 minutes, or until chips become shiny and soft. Spread to cover and let cool slightly. Cut into bars about 2 by 1 $^3\!/_4$ inches. Cool completely.
5. For topping, combine confectioners' sugar, 2 tablespoons Jif peanut butter and evaporated milk. Stir until well blended. Drizzle over chocolate. Sprinkle with toffee bits, if desired. Makes 24 bars.

* Brands may vary by region; substitute a similar product.

Desserts

Blueberry Coffee Cake
GROWER DIRECT/
WESTERN SWEET CHERRY ▼

CAKE
1/4 cup salad oil
2 ounces cream cheese, softened
1 egg, beaten
1/2 cup half-and-half
1 1/2 cups sifted all-purpose flour
3/4 cup sugar
2 teaspoons baking powder
1/2 teaspoon salt

TOPPING
1/3 cup packed light brown sugar
1 tablespoon all-purpose flour
1/2 teaspoon ground cinnamon
1/2 teaspoon grated nutmeg
1/2 cup broken pecans
1 tablespoon butter, melted
3/4 cup fresh Grower Direct*
   blueberries (or thawed frozen)

1. Preheat oven to 375°F.

2. To prepare the cake, combine salad oil, cream cheese, egg and half-and-half in a bowl and mix well.

3. In another bowl, sift together flour, sugar, baking powder and salt. Add to the wet ingredients and mix well.

4. To prepare the topping, combine brown sugar, flour, cinnamon, nutmeg, pecans and melted butter in a bowl.

5. Pour the cake batter into a greased 9-by-9-by-2-inch pan. Spread blueberries evenly over the batter. Sprinkle evenly with the topping. Bake for 30-35 minutes, or until a toothpick inserted in the center comes out clean. Makes 8 servings.

Brands may vary by region; substitute a similar product.

The Ultimate Carrot Cake
GRIMMWAY FARMS ▲

2 cups sifted flour
2 teaspoons baking powder
1 1/2 teaspoons baking soda
1 1/2 teaspoons salt
2 teaspoons cinnamon
2 cups sugar
1 1/2 cups canola oil
4 eggs
2 cups peeled and finely grated Grimmway* carrots
1 8-ounce can crushed pineapple, drained

1/2 cup chopped nuts (optional)
1 3 1/2-ounce can flaked coconut
Coconut, for garnish (optional)

CREAM CHEESE FROSTING

1/2 cup unsalted butter, softened
1 8-ounce package cream cheese, softened
1 teaspoon vanilla extract
1 pound confectioners' sugar

1. Preheat oven to 350°F.

2. Sift together flour, baking powder, baking soda, salt and cinnamon. Add sugar, oil and eggs; mix well. Add carrots, pineapple, nuts and coconut; blend thoroughly. Pour into 3 greased and floured 9-inch round cake pans.

3. Bake for 25-30 minutes, or until a toothpick inserted in the center comes out clean (don't overcook). Cool in pans for a few minutes, then remove and let cool on a wire rack.

4. To make the frosting, beat butter, cream cheese and vanilla until creamy. Gradually beat in sugar. If too thick, add a small amount of milk. Frost the cake. Sprinkle with coconut, if desired. Makes 8-10 servings.

* Brands may vary by region; substitute a similar product.

Easy Carrot Cake
BOLTHOUSE FARMS ▲

1 package (2-layer size) spice cake mix
2 cups grated Bolthouse Farms* carrots (about 1/2 pound)
1 8-ounce can crushed pineapple, drained
1 cup chopped pecans, divided
2 8-ounce packages cream cheese, softened
2 cups confectioners' sugar
1 8-ounce tub whipped dessert topping, thawed

1. Preheat oven to 350°F.

2. Prepare cake mix as directed on package, stirring carrots, pineapple and 3/4 cup of the pecans into the batter until well blended. Pour into 2 prepared 9-inch round baking pans. Bake for 25-30 minutes, or until a toothpick inserted in the center comes out clean. Cool.

3. Meanwhile, beat cream cheese and sugar with an electric mixer or a wire whisk until well blended. Stir in whipped topping until well blended.

4. Place 1 cake layer on a serving plate. Spread with 1 1/2 cups of cream cheese mixture. Carefully place second cake layer on top of the first. Frost top and sides of cake with remaining cream cheese mixture. Garnish with remaining 1/4 cup pecans. Refrigerate until ready to serve. Makes 16 servings.

* Brands may vary by region; substitute a similar product.

Desserts ▌

Pound Cake Tiramisu
BEST BRANDS/MULTIFOODS ▼

1 Kirkland Signature bakery-fresh pound cake
1/2 cup cold brewed coffee
3 tablespoons coffee liqueur
8 ounces cream cheese, room temperature
1/3 cup sugar
2 tablespoons Nescafé Ice Java chocolate mocha syrup
2 tablespoons milk
Crushed English toffee or chocolate-covered coffee beans, for garnish

Best Brands Corp.

1. Lay pound cake on its side. Cut the entire cake lengthwise into quarters. Place pieces side by side in a 9-by-13-inch glass baking dish.

2. Combine cold coffee and 2 tablespoons coffee liqueur. Using a toothpick or thin skewer, poke holes in the cake. Drizzle the coffee mixture evenly over the cake.

3. Using an electric mixer, beat together cream cheese and sugar, then beat in mocha syrup and 1 tablespoon coffee liqueur, and then milk. After the milk is incorporated, beat at high speed until the mixture is light and fluffy, about 1 minute.

4. Spread cream cheese mixture over the prepared pound cake. Serve immediately or refrigerate, covered, for up to 24 hours.

5. To serve, cut into squares and top with choice of garnish.
Makes 12 servings.

Banana Chocolate Tea Bread
BONITA BANANA ▲

1/2 cup butter, softened

1 cup sugar

2 eggs

1 1/2 cups all-purpose flour

2 tablespoons cocoa

1 teaspoon baking soda

1 teaspoon salt

1/2 teaspoon ground cinnamon

1 teaspoon vanilla extract

1 cup mashed Bonita* bananas

1/2 cup sour cream

1/3 cup chopped walnuts

1/3 cup miniature semisweet chocolate morsels

1. Preheat oven to 350°F.

2. Cream butter; gradually add sugar, beating until light and fluffy. Add eggs one at a time, beating well after each addition.

3. Combine flour, cocoa, baking soda, salt and cinnamon; sift together. Stir flour mixture into egg mixture, blending well. Add vanilla. Stir in banana, sour cream, walnuts and chocolate morsels.

4. Spoon batter into 2 greased and floured 3-by-7 1/2-inch loaf pans. Bake for 55 minutes, or until a toothpick inserted in the center comes out clean.

5. Cool in pans for 10 minutes, then remove and cool completely on a wire rack. Makes 2 loaves.

Brands may vary by region; substitute a similar product.

Banana Cupcakes with Belgian Chunk Cookie Bottom
BARRY CALLEBAUT ▲

2 1/2 cups flour

1 1/2 teaspoons baking powder

1 teaspoon baking soda

1 teaspoon salt

1 cup vegetable shortening

1 1/2 cups sugar

3/4 cup milk

2 eggs

1 cup mashed banana

1 tablespoon lemon juice

1 teaspoon vanilla extract

8 Kirkland Signature chocolate chunk cookies, crushed (the Belgian chocolate chunks are from Barry Callebaut)

1. Preheat oven to 350°F.

2. In a bowl, sift together flour, baking powder, baking soda and salt.

3. In another bowl, beat together shortening and sugar with an electric mixer. Add milk, eggs, banana, lemon juice and vanilla; mix to combine well. Add the sifted dry ingredients and mix just until smooth.

4. Place crushed cookies in 24 greased muffin cups and top with the banana mixture. Bake for 25-35 minutes, or until a toothpick comes out clean. Makes 24 servings.

Caramel Pumpkin Cake
KRUSTEAZ ▲

1 16-ounce package Krusteaz Pumpkin Spice Quick Bread Mix*
1/2 cup water
1/3 cup vegetable oil
2 eggs
1/2 cup butterscotch chips
1/4 cup caramel sauce, plus more for garnish
Whipped cream

1. Preheat oven to 350°F. Lightly grease a 9-inch cake pan.
2. In a medium bowl, stir together quick bread mix, water, oil, eggs and butterscotch chips. Spoon batter into the prepared pan.
3. Drizzle 1/4 cup caramel sauce over the batter. Swirl with a knife in the shape of large circles.
4. Bake for 30-35 minutes, or until a toothpick inserted in the center comes out clean. Let the cake cool in the pan for 15 minutes, then gently loosen from the pan and transfer to a wire rack. Cool completely.
5. Garnish with fresh whipped cream and warmed caramel sauce, if desired. Makes 8 servings.

Brands may vary by region; substitute a similar product.

KRUSTEAZ®

Red, White and Blueberry Cheesecake
JON DONAIRE ▲

1/4 cup (1/2 stick) unsalted butter
1/4 cup sugar
2 cups frozen raspberries
2 cups frozen blueberries
1 Jon Donaire* Baked New York Cheesecake

GARNISH
Whipped cream
Raspberries
Blueberries
Fresh mint leaves

1. Melt butter in a heavy skillet over high heat. Mix in sugar. Add frozen berries and stir until berries are heated through, about 3 minutes. Remove from heat and let stand for approximately 10 minutes.
2. Place a thawed slice of cheesecake on a dessert plate. Spoon 2 tablespoons of warm sauce over cheesecake slice. Garnish with a rosette of whipped cream. Place a raspberry, blueberry and mint leaf in the rosette. Serve immediately. Makes 16 servings.

Brands may vary by region; substitute a similar product.

RICH'S
Jon Donaire
DESSERTS

Croissant Cream Cheese Flan
KIRKLAND SIGNATURE/PURATOS ▼

4 Kirkland Signature croissants
1 1/2 cups sugar, divided
5 large eggs
8 ounces cream cheese, softened
18 ounces evaporated milk
7 ounces sweetened condensed milk
16 ounces half-and-half
1 tablespoon vanilla extract

1. Preheat oven to 350°F.

2. Slice croissants in half and lightly toast in the oven, face up, for 10 minutes.

3. Caramelize the bottom of an 8-by-4-inch round pan by pouring 1/2 cup sugar into the pan. Dissolve the sugar over medium heat until light brown, making sure to cover the entire bottom of the pan. Let cool.

4. Layer toasted croissants in the pan.

5. In a blender, mix eggs for 2 minutes. Add cream cheese, evaporated milk and condensed milk; blend to obtain a creamy custard.

6. Pour egg mixture into a large bowl and add remaining sugar, half-and-half and vanilla. Mix with a wooden spoon until well incorporated and pour over croissants. Make sure the mixture saturates the croissants.

7. Place the pan in a larger pan containing 1/2 inch of warm water and bake for about 1 hour. Cooking time may vary depending on the oven. Flan should have a light golden color when done.

8. Remove from the oven and let cool. Refrigerate for 4 hours before serving. Makes 10 servings.

Tip: Cut flan into squares and serve with a scoop of your favorite ice cream on top. Drizzle with caramel sauce from the pan and you have a delicious flan à la mode.

Reliable partners in innovation

Desserts I

Chuck's Jonagold Apple Cake
HOLTZINGER FRUIT ▲

2 cups sifted flour
2 teaspoons baking soda
1 teaspoon salt
1 teaspoon grated nutmeg
1 teaspoon ground cinnamon
2 cups granulated sugar
1/2 cup butter or margarine, softened
2 eggs
4 cups peeled, chopped Holtzinger Fruit* Jonagold apples
Brown sugar

1. Preheat oven to 350°F.
2. In a bowl, sift together flour, baking soda, salt, nutmeg and cinnamon.
3. In another bowl, cream granulated sugar, butter and eggs. Add to dry mixture. Add apples and stir to combine.
4. Pour batter into a buttered 9-by-13-inch pan. Sprinkle with brown sugar.
5. Bake for 45-60 minutes, or until a toothpick inserted in the center comes out clean. Makes 12 servings.

Brands may vary by region; substitute a similar product.

Cherry-Almond Yogurt Dessert Bars
YOPLAIT ▲

1 cup sliced almonds, toasted
1 9-ounce package chocolate wafer cookies, finely crushed
1/3 cup butter or stick margarine, melted
3 6-ounce containers Yoplait Original 99% Fat Free or Light Fat Free strawberry yogurt
1 12-ounce jar cherry preserves (1 cup)
1/2 teaspoon almond extract or vanilla extract
1 8-ounce container frozen light whipped dessert topping, thawed
1/2 cup chocolate syrup

1. In a blender or food processor, finely grind 1/3 cup of the almonds.
2. In a medium bowl, stir together crushed cookies, ground almonds and melted butter. Press mixture firmly into the bottom of an ungreased 9-by-13-inch pan. Freeze for about 10 minutes, or until firm.
3. In a large bowl, stir together yogurt, preserves and almond extract. Gently stir in whipped topping. Spread yogurt mixture over cookie mixture in pan. Cover and freeze for 3 hours, or until firm.
4. Let stand at room temperature for 10 minutes, then cut into 20 bars.
5. To serve, drizzle each bar with chocolate syrup and sprinkle with sliced almonds. Makes 20 servings.

Upside-Down Mango Ginger Cake
READY PAC ▼

1 32-ounce package Ready Pac* fresh mango
2 tablespoons frozen orange juice concentrate, thawed
2 teaspoons fresh lime juice
3 tablespoons butter
¼ cup packed brown sugar
1 14 ½-ounce box gingerbread mix
¾ cup chilled whipping cream
¼ cup sour cream
1 tablespoon confectioners' sugar

1. Preheat oven to 350°F.

2. Combine 12 mango slices, orange juice concentrate and lime juice in a large bowl. Toss to mix and let stand for 10 minutes.

3. Place butter in a 9-by-2-inch round cake pan and put in the oven until butter is melted. Remove from the oven and sprinkle brown sugar over butter. Arrange mango slices in an attractive pattern over sugar.

4. Prepare gingerbread according to package directions; pour batter over mangoes. Bake for 35-40 minutes, or until a toothpick inserted in the center comes out clean. Let cool for 5 minutes, then invert on a platter.

5. Meanwhile, place cream in a small chilled bowl. Whip with an electric mixer on high speed until stiff peaks form. By hand, whisk in sour cream and confectioners' sugar.

6. To serve, cut cake in wedges and top with a dollop of whipped cream mixture. Serve warm or at room temperature. Makes 8 servings.

* Brands may vary by region; substitute a similar product.

Chocolate Muffin Bread Pudding with Cherry Sauce
BEST BRANDS/MULTIFOODS ▲

2 Kirkland Signature bakery-fresh chocolate muffins
2 eggs
1/4 cup sugar
1 teaspoon vanilla extract
2 cups (1 pint) half-and-half
1/2 cup chopped dried tart cherries
Whipped cream, for garnish

CHERRY SAUCE
1 cup dried tart cherries
1/4 cup kirsch
3/4 cup water
3/4 cup cherry preserves

1. Prepare Cherry Sauce: Combine all ingredients in a saucepan and bring to a boil, stirring. Continue to boil, stirring, for 2 minutes. Let cool. Refrigerate, covered, to thicken.
2. Preheat oven to 350°F.
3. Cut each muffin into 15-20 cubes. Place in a single layer on a pan and bake for 15 minutes. Let cool.
4. Place eggs, sugar, vanilla and half-and-half in a bowl and whisk until blended. Stir in muffin cubes and cherries. Let sit for 10 minutes, stirring occasionally so pieces absorb liquid.
5. Pour into a greased 9-by-9-inch glass baking dish. Bake for 35-45 minutes, or until knife inserted in the center comes out clean.
6. To serve, place small scoops of pudding in bowls, goblets or parfait glasses. Top with Cherry Sauce and whipped cream. Makes 6-9 servings.

Best Brands Corp.

Chocolate Molten Lava Brownie Bites
SUGAR BOWL BAKERY ▲

1 1/2 cups semisweet chocolate chips
1 cup heavy cream
2 tablespoons butter
1 16-ounce zipper-lock bag
1 3-pound container Sugar Bowl Bakery* Brownie Bites**
Fresh fruit, for garnish
Confectioners' sugar, for garnish

1. Place chocolate chips in a metal bowl. Heat cream to a simmer. Pour over chocolate chips and whisk until smooth. Add butter and whisk until incorporated.
2. Pour chocolate into zipper-lock bag and refrigerate until firm to the touch.
3. Using a wooden dowel or chopstick, punch a 1/2-inch hole in the underside of each brownie.
4. When chocolate is firm, snip off one of the bottom corners of the bag. Pipe 2 tablespoons of filling into each brownie hole.
5. Place up to 5 brownies, with the hole facing up, on a plate; heat on high in the microwave for approximately 10 seconds.
6. Remove to clean plates and split the brownies in half, allowing the chocolate to flow. Garnish with fresh fruit and confectioners' sugar. Makes 46 pieces.

* Brands may vary by region; substitute a similar product.
** 2-pound containers are available in selected regions. Adjust recipe accordingly.

Oooey-Gooey Popcorn Pull
CONAGRA

2 3 1/2-ounce bags Orville Redenbacher's Microwave Gourmet
   Popping Corn
1 1/2 cups cashews (8 ounces)
1 6-ounce package sweetened dried cranberries (about 1 1/4 cups)
2 cups maple-flavored syrup
1 tablespoon cider vinegar
1/4 cup (1/2 stick) Fleischmann's Original Margarine
2 teaspoons vanilla extract

1. Microwave popcorn according to package directions. Remove unpopped
kernels. Place in a 6-quart bowl. Add cashews and cranberries; mix lightly.
Set aside.
2. Cover a baking sheet with parchment paper; set aside.
3. Mix syrup and vinegar in a *deep* saucepan until well blended. (Saucepan
must be deep to prevent syrup from boiling over the edge.) Bring to a boil
over high heat. Continue boiling until the temperature reaches 250°F on a
candy thermometer, or until a small amount dropped into very cold water
forms a firm ball that does not flatten when removed from the water (about
15-20 minutes total). Remove from heat. Blend in margarine and vanilla.
4. Drizzle hot syrup immediately over popcorn mixture. Carefully toss with
spatulas until popcorn is well coated. Spread onto the prepared baking sheet;
cool before serving. Store leftovers in an airtight container.
Makes 16 servings (about 1 cup each).
Popcorn Bars: Grease a 9-by-13-inch baking pan with additional
margarine. Toss popcorn mixture with hot syrup mixture as directed,
then press firmly into the pan with a spatula or the back of a spoon.
Cool completely. Cut into 16 bars to serve.

ConAgra
Foods.

Sugar Cookies
OREGON CHAI ▲

1 cup butter, softened
1 cup granulated sugar
1 egg
3 tablespoons Oregon Chai* The Original concentrate
2 1/2 cups flour
1 teaspoon baking powder

FROSTING
3 cups confectioners' sugar
1/3 cup butter, softened
2-4 tablespoons Oregon Chai* concentrate
Sugar sprinkles (optional)

1. To make the cookies, combine butter, sugar, egg and chai concentrate in a large bowl. Beat until creamy. Add flour and baking powder and beat until well blended. Divide dough into 2 pieces, cover and refrigerate until firm (2-3 hours or overnight).

2. Preheat oven to 400°F.

3. On a lightly floured surface, roll out dough to 1/4-inch thickness. Cut out cookies with a cookie cutter. Place on an ungreased cookie sheet. Bake 6-10 minutes, or until lightly browned. Cool completely on a wire rack.

4. To make the frosting, blend confectioners' sugar, butter and chai concentrate in a bowl. Beat, adding more concentrate if necessary for desired consistency. Frost the cooled cookies. Makes 6 dozen cookies.

* Brands may vary by region; substitute a similar product.

Cookie Surprise
SNICKERS ▲

2 sticks butter (8 ounces), softened
1 cup creamy peanut butter
1 cup light brown sugar
1 cup granulated sugar
2 eggs
1 teaspoon vanilla extract
3 1/2 cups all-purpose flour, sifted
1 teaspoon baking soda
1/2 teaspoon salt
1 bag Snickers Brand Miniatures

1. Beat together butter, peanut butter and sugars with an electric mixer on medium to low speed until light and fluffy.

2. Slowly add eggs and vanilla until thoroughly combined. Then mix in flour, baking soda and salt.

3. Cover and chill dough for 2-3 hours.

4. Preheat oven to 325°F.

5. Divide dough into 1-tablespoon pieces and flatten. Place a Snickers Miniature in the center of each piece of dough. Form dough into a ball around the candy.

6. Place on a greased cookie sheet and bake for 10-12 minutes. Let cookies cool on a baking rack or on waxed paper. Makes 24 cookies.

Nest Cookies
JELLY BELLY ▼

1 1/2 cups all-purpose flour
1 teaspoon baking powder
1/2 teaspoon salt
1/2 cup shortening
1/2 cup sugar
1 egg white
1 teaspoon vanilla extract
2 tablespoons milk
2 cups shredded coconut
6 ounces Jelly Belly jelly beans (assorted flavors)

1. Preheat oven to 375°F.

2. Sift together flour, baking powder and salt; set aside.

3. In a large bowl, beat shortening, sugar, egg white and vanilla until well blended. Add flour mixture and milk and beat until blended. Stir in coconut.

4. Roll dough into a ball and divide in half. Roll fifteen 1-inch balls from each half and place on an ungreased baking sheet. Make a thumbprint impression in the center of each ball to form a nest. Bake for 6 minutes.

5. Remove from the oven and place 4-5 jelly beans in the center of each cookie. Bake for 5 more minutes, taking care that the jelly beans don't melt.

6. Transfer cookies to a wire rack to cool. Makes 30 cookies.

Beverages

Refreshing Summer Smoothie
FOUR STAR FRUIT ◀

12 Four Star Fruit seedless red grapes
1 6-ounce container vanilla yogurt
1/2 cup vanilla ice cream
1 tablespoon honey
1 cup ice cubes

In a blender, combine grapes, yogurt, ice cream, honey and ice.
Blend until smooth. Makes 2 servings.

Very Very Berry Smoothie
DANNON ▲

3/4 cup (6 ounces) Dannon* Light 'n Fit Strawberry Yogurt
3/4 cup (5 ounces) mixed frozen berries (strawberries, raspberries,
    blueberries) or 3/4 cup fresh berries and 1 cup crushed ice
1 banana, peeled and cut in chunks

Place all ingredients in a blender; process until smooth and serve
immediately. Makes 1 serving.

Brands may vary by region; substitute a similar product.

Strawberry Smoothie
KIRKLAND SIGNATURE
SILK/CLIFFSTAR ▲

10 ounces Kirkland Signature/Silk Vanilla Soymilk
10 ounces Kirkland Signature Cranberry Cocktail
2 cups Sunrise Growers frozen strawberries
8 ounces Kirkland Signature strawberry yogurt

Place all ingredients in a blender. Blend until smooth.
Makes 2-3 servings.

Tip: For a thicker smoothie, substitute 1 fresh banana for 1 cup of the strawberries.

Berry Smoothie
KIRKLAND SIGNATURE
CLIFFSTAR/SILK ▲

10 ounces Kirkland Signature/Silk Vanilla Soymilk
10 ounces Kirkland Signature Cranberry-Raspberry Juice
2 cups Nature's Three Berries (frozen)
8 ounces Kirkland Signature blueberry yogurt

Place all ingredients in a blender. Blend until smooth.
Makes 2-3 servings.

Yakima Iced Apple Tea
TREE TOP

6 tea bags
¹/₄ teaspoon ground allspice
¹/₃ cup honey
3 cups Tree Top* Apple Juice
Lemon slices (optional)

1. Bring 3 cups of cold water to a boil in a saucepan. Remove from heat and add tea bags to the boiling water. Let stand for 5 minutes.

2. Remove tea bags. Add allspice, honey and apple juice. Simmer over low heat until honey is blended, about 1 minute.

3. Let cool and then chill. Serve over ice with lemon slices.

Makes 6 servings.

* Brands may vary by region; substitute a similar product.

Marvelous Mint Crush
SWEET'N LOW

¹/₂ cup fresh mint leaves, washed and dried, torn in half
1 ¹/₃ tablespoons or 12 packets Sweet'N Low* Zero Calorie Sweetener
3 cups cold water
¹/₂ cup freshly squeezed lemon juice
1 ¹/₂ cups club soda
Fresh mint leaves, for garnish (optional)

1. Place mint leaves in the bottom of a pitcher. Add Sweet'N Low and crush mixture with the back of a wooden spoon.

2. Add water, lemon juice and club soda; stir.

3. Serve immediately over crushed ice in glasses, garnished with fresh mint leaves, if desired. Makes 4 servings.

* Brands may vary by region; substitute a similar product.

Coffee Latte
EQUAL ▲

1 1/4 cups regular-grind espresso or other dark-roast ground coffee
1 cinnamon stick, broken into pieces
6 cups water
8 packets Equal sweetener
2 1/2 cups fat-free milk
Ground cinnamon or nutmeg

1. Place ground coffee and cinnamon stick in the filter basket of a drip coffee pot. Add water and brew the coffee.

2. Stir Equal into the pot of coffee. Pour coffee into 8 mugs or cups.

3. Heat milk in a small saucepan until steaming.

4. Pour half of milk into a blender container, cover and process at high speed until foamy, about 15 seconds. Pour into coffee mugs. Repeat with the remaining milk.

5. Sprinkle with cinnamon or nutmeg before serving. Makes 8 servings.

Tips: This recipe is 49% lower in calories than the traditional drink. Pour it over ice for a refreshing summer drink.

Ruby Red Citrus Warmer
APPLE & EVE ▲

1/2 cup sugar
1 cup pineapple juice
3 cups Apple & Eve* Ruby Red Grapefruit Juice Cocktail
1 cup Apple & Eve* Naturally Cranberry Juice
Bitters, to taste
1/2 cup dark rum (or substitute 1 cup Apple & Eve* Natural Style Apple Juice for a nonalcoholic version)
Cinnamon sticks, for garnish
Grapefruit slices, for garnish

1. In a large saucepan, dissolve sugar in pineapple juice over low heat.

2. Add grapefruit juice and cranberry juice and bring to a slow simmer; do not boil.

3. Remove from heat and add bitters and rum. Serve warm, garnished with cinnamon sticks and grapefruit slices. Makes 6-7 servings.

* Brands may vary by region; substitute a similar product.

Spicy Mayan Mocha
SAN FRANCISCO BAY ▼

¹/₂ cup whipping cream

³/₄ teaspoon ground cinnamon, divided

¹/₄ teaspoon grated nutmeg

1 tablespoon sugar

1 ¹/₂ cups freshly brewed San Francisco Bay* coffee

4 teaspoons chocolate syrup

1. In a mixing bowl, combine whipping cream, ¹/₄ teaspoon cinnamon, nutmeg and sugar. Whip until soft peaks form.

2. Place remaining ¹/₂ teaspoon cinnamon in the pot of coffee and stir.

3. Pour 1 teaspoon chocolate syrup into each of 4 coffee mugs.

4. Pour coffee into the mugs and stir in the chocolate syrup.

5. Top each mug with the spicy whipped cream. Add a shot of rum if desired. Makes 4 servings.

* Brands may vary by region; substitute a similar product.

ENJOY THE PERFECT CUP OF COFFEE AT HOME

You're off to a good start by selecting high-quality, perfectly roasted beans from Starbucks. But there's more to great coffee than picking the right beans. You'll also need to store, grind and brew those beans properly. The good news: this is all very easy.

1. **Match the correct grind to your coffeemaker.**

   The coffee-brewing method you use at home – press, drip or espresso – dictates how finely your coffee should be ground. Coffee presses require a coarse grind. Espresso machines require a very fine grind. Drip coffeemakers fall in between those two.

2. **Proportion is important.**

   Too much water, and you have a weak brew. Too little, and you may find it undrinkable. We recommend 2 Tbsp (10g) ground coffee for every 6 fl oz (180mL) of water. If you decide that's too strong, you can always add hot water after brewing.

3. **Use fresh, cold water.**

   With so much attention paid to selecting and grinding the beans, it's easy to forget the importance of good water. The water you have at home should be clean, fresh and free of impurities. If your local tap water isn't up to snuff, then consider filtered or bottled water.

4. **Proper storage will help maintain the freshness and flavor of your coffee.**

   Coffee is an agricultural product which means it will be at the peak of freshness for only about a week after the FlavorLock™ bag is opened. You can keep your coffee fresher (and tasting better) longer by storing whole beans in a dry, dark place. An airtight, opaque container kept at room temperature is best.

5. **Serve coffee at the peak of flavor and freshness.**

   Boiling produces bitter coffee; it should be brewed between 195°F and 205°F (90°C and 96°C) to extract the full range of flavors. After brewing, you can keep it on a burner for only 20 minutes or so before it becomes unpleasant. A thermal carafe will keep coffee hot and delicious for much longer periods of time. And never reheat coffee – that just makes it taste bad.

WITH THE RIGHT COFFEE AND THE PROPER TECHNIQUES, YOU'RE ON YOUR WAY TO BREWING THE PERFECT CUP.

I A

Ahi tuna
>   grilled, sesame-crusted,
>   in ginger soy marinade, 119

Apples
>   baked, with granola, 159
>   baked, with hazelnut and orange, 158
>   cake, Jonagold, 176
>   crisp, "good for you," 161
>   dumplings, 161
>   in greens with cherry vinaigrette, 39
>   juice, in iced tea, 185
>   juice, in ruby red citrus warmer, 186
>   pie, 162
>   salad, crab, 38
>   strudel, 160

Artichokes with ricotta and basil, 64

Asparagus
>   cashew-topped, 63
>   enchiladas, 147
>   risotto with tomatoes, 103

Avocados
>   salad, fruit stand, 44
>   salad, grape tomato and, 46
>   salad, mango and, 46
>   salad, orange and black olive, 43
>   salad, pasta and bell pepper with
>   feta cheese, 45
>   salad, red grape, grape tomato and, 105

I B

Bacon
>   in baked beans, 82
>   in easy cheesy potatoes, 59
>   in Spinach and Potatoes au Gratin, 61
>   in western bean salad, 48
>   -wrapped marinated pork loin, 81
>   -wrapped shrimp, 25

Bacon bits, prepared, in pork tenderloin with
>   cilantro lime pesto, 83

Bagel Bites (ingredient), with
>   dipping sauce, 35

Bagels, prepared, in
>   Denver omelet panini, 13

Bananas
>   bread, chocolate, 173

bread, coffee, 21
cupcakes with cookie bottom, 173
in festive party salad, 41

Barbecue sauce, prepared, in classic baby
>   back ribs, 129

Bars
>   cherry-almond yogurt, 176
>   chocolatey peanut butter, 169
>   harvest fruit, 23

Beans, canned
>   baked, "Angus" style, with applewood-
>   smoked bacon and kielbasa, 82
>   salad, western, 48
>   in salsa, corn and black bean, 32

Beans, green, sauté, 65

Beef
>   bourguignon, 128
>   burgers, BBQ, in lettuce wraps, 150
>   burgers, cheese, 151
>   eye of round with roasted
>   vegetables, 127
>   filet mignon, in sweet onion
>   Napoleon, 150
>   kabobs, teriyaki, with pineapple
>   sesame rice, 74
>   pot roast, Sicilian-style, 101
>   prime rib, garlic-studded, 126
>   roast, prepared, in French dip, 101
>   sirloin, in quesadillas, 33
>   steaks, porterhouse or T-bone, with
>   Parmesan-grilled vegetables, 127

Berries, frozen, in smoothie, 184

Beverages
>   citrus warmer, ruby red, 186
>   mint crush, 185
>   tea, iced apple, 185

Bisquick (ingredient), in
>   sausage-cheese balls, 34

Blueberries
>   coffee cake, 170
>   crumble, double berry, 159
>   dried, in cheese spread, 30
>   fruit salad, and mango, 103
>   tart, two-berry, with chocolate
>   drizzle, 165

Bread
>   banana chocolate, 173
>   Bing cherry cream cheese nut, 21
>   coffee banana, 21
>   garlic, prepared, in spinach blue cheese
>   flatbread, 34
>   mix, in caramel pumpkin cake, 174
>   multi-grain (ingredient), in
>   French toast, 16

Breakfast knots, orange and apple, 19

Broccoli
>   in Chinese noodle and
>   vegetable salad, 49
>   with maple-sesame dressing, 52

Brownie bites, prepared, chocolate
>   molten lava, 178

I C

Cakes
>   apple, Jonagold, 176
>   blueberry coffee, 170
>   caramel pumpkin, 174
>   carrot, 171
>   carrot, easy, 171
>   mango ginger, upside-down, 177

Cantaloupe
>   in fruit bowl with raspberry
>   vinaigrette, 20
>   in fruit salad, tropical, 43

Carrots
>   cake, 171
>   cake, easy, 171

Cashew-topped asparagus, 63

Catfish, sautéed, with sliced lettuce
>   Niçoise, 125

Chai, prepared, in sugar cookies, 180

Cheese
>   Cheddar, sauce, with salmon
>   and pasta, 115
>   cottage, in bacon and Cheddar
>   omelet roll, 13
>   mozzarella, fresh, in grilled pineapple
>   and ham skewers, 35
>   Parmesan, in eggplant gratin, 144
>   Parmesan, primavera pasta pie, 141
>   provolone, in eggplant gratin, 144

ricotta, in eggplant gratin, 144

spread, red, white and blueberry, 30

Cheesecake, prepared, red, white and
blueberry, 174

Cherries

bread, cream cheese nut, 21

compote, 155

in greens with cherry vinaigrette, 39

salad, with greens, 37

salad, picnic, 37

Chicken

in agnolotti, 80

in angel hair pasta with tomato cream
sauce, 143

balsamic, and pears, 134

Black Forest, skillet, 135

cracker jack, 85

cream topping, mushroom, 133

crispy bits, 85

drumsticks, hunter's style, 79

with mangoes, 138

Monterey, 135

pecan-crusted, with honey-mustard
sauce, 134

roulade with bacon, 136

salad, Grand Parisian, 136

salad, and pear, 40

salpicón, chipotle, 71

stir-fried lemon, 133

Thai, tangy, 70

thighs with saffron, green olives
and mint, 79

wings, Tex-Mex, with pico de gallo, 70

Chicken, prepared

frozen mesquite grilled, in pizza, 138

rotisserie, in stir-fry, 137

Chicken pot pie, prepared, with
crabmeat-stuffed mushrooms, 139

Chili, monster, 149

Chimichangas, prepared, with grilled
vegetables, 146

Ciabatta rolls, prepared, in ham and
avocado torta, 153

Clams, canned, in gazpacho, 53

Clementines, delicious, 156

Cod, Tuscan, 121

Coffee

bread, banana, 21

how to brew, 188

latte, 186

mocha, spicy, 187

Cookies

nest, 181

sugar, with chai, 180

surprise, 180

Cookies, prepared

brownie bites, chocolate molten
lava, 178

chocolate chunk, in banana
cupcakes, 173

oatmeal raisin, in pancakes, 17

Corn

canned, in salsa, black bean, 32

chowder, lobster, 94

relish, roasted, 149

salsa, 124

Cottage cheese, in bacon and Cheddar
omelet roll, 13

Couscous, almond, 87

Crab

cakes, Dungeness, 26

king, with Chardonnay beurre
blanc sauce, 108

legs, Dungeness, marinated, 109

melt, spicy, 26

in Napoleon, sweet onion beef, 150

in potatoes, twice-baked, 59

salad, apple, 38

scampi, 108

Crackers, prepared, in tomato crostini, 31

Cranberry cocktail, in strawberry
smoothie, 184

Cranberry juice, in ruby red citrus
warmer, 186

Cranberry-raspberry juice, in
berry smoothie, 184

Cream cheese

in cucumber dip, 29

in red, white and blueberry spread, 30

Crisp

apple, "good for you," 161

peach, 155

Croissants, prepared

cream cheese flan, 175

grilled, with orange caramel sauce, 18

melt, 13

Cucumbers

dip, 29

in gazpacho, 53

in sea scallops on summer succotash, 96

I D

Dates, stuffed Medjool, 166

Desserts. See also Cakes; Cookies; Pies; Tarts

ambrosia, Florida, 157

apples, baked, with granola, 159

apples, baked, with hazelnut
and orange, 158

Asian pears with gingered
pluot sauce, 157

bars, cherry-almond yogurt, 176

bars, chocolatey peanut butter, 169

bread pudding, chocolate muffin, with
cherry sauce, 178

cheesecake, red, white and blueberry, 174

chocolate molten lava brownie bites, 178

clementines, delicious, 156

compote, cherry, 155

crisp, apple, "good for you," 161

crisp, peach, 155

crumble, double berry, 159

cupcakes, banana, with Belgian chunk
cookie bottom, 173

dates, stuffed Medjool, 166

dumplings, apple, 161

flan, croissant cream cheese, 175

frozen grape and lemon treats, 167

fruit pizza, 163

galette, rustic peach, 168

granita, red grape white wine, 105

popcorn pull, 179

rugala martini, 168

sorbet, mango, 166

strudel, apple, 160

tiramisu, pound cake, 172

Dipping sauces for sushi, 28

Dips

artichoke, 30

cucumber, 29
shrimp, 29

I E

Egg Starts (ingredient), in strawberry and
      ricotta cheese omelet, 11
Eggplant gratin, 144
Eggs
      in bacon and Cheddar omelet roll, 13
      in breakfast casserole, 15
      in breakfast tostada with Eggo
          waffles, 14
      in croissant melt, 11
      in Denver omelet bagel panini, 13
Enchiladas, asparagus, 147
Energy drink, in monster chili, 149
English muffin, prepared, in club
      sandwich, 152

I F

Flatbread, garlic, prepared, spinach
      blue cheese, 34
Flautas, prepared, with spicy mango salsa, 33
Flounder, pan-fried almond &
      Parmesan-crusted, 120
Franks with roasted corn relish, 149
French toast
      healthy, 16
      soufflé, 16
Fruit, prepared fresh, in dessert pizza, 163
Fruit salad. See Salad

I G

Grapefruit
      in ambrosia, Florida, 157
      in citrus salad with grilled shrimp
          adobo, 110
      juice, in ruby red citrus warmer, 186
Grapes
      in fresh fruit tart, 164
      frozen, and lemon treats, 167
      in fruit bowl with raspberry
          vinaigrette, 20
      granita, red grape white wine, 105
      in salad, festive party, 41
      salad, red grape, grape tomato and

avocado, 105
smoothie, 183

I H

Half-and-half, in bacon and Cheddar
      omelet roll, 13
Ham
      Black Forest, in chicken skillet, 135
      spiral cut, in Hawaiian wraps, 82
Hommus, prepared, in quesadillas, 33
Honeydew melon, in fruit bowl with
      raspberry vinaigrette, 20
Hot Pockets (ingredient), with salad, 148

I J

Jambalaya, Louisiana hot sausage, 148
Jarlsberg sunset salad, 50
Jelly beans, in nest cookies, 181

I K

Ketchup, prepared, in chicken Monterey, 135
Kielbasa, in baked beans, 82

I L

Lahvash, in prepared flatbread rollers, 50
Lamb
      leg, orange and apricot, with
          almond couscous, 87
      rack, with rosemary mustard cream, 87
      tandoori, with cumin sauce, 88
Lasagna, prepared, with minestrone, 55
Lemon, stir-fried, chicken, 133
Lettuce
      iceberg, in Chinese noodle and
          vegetable salad, 49
      iceberg wraps, BBQ burgers in, 150
      romaine, in Chinese noodle and
          vegetable salad, 49
      romaine, in fruit salad, 41
      romaine, in layered salad, 47
Lobster chowder, roasted corn and, 94

I M

Mangoes
      cake, upside-down, ginger, 177
      dried, chicken with, 138
      fruit salad, and blueberry, 103

in fruit salad, tropical, 43
      salad, avocado, 46
      salsa, spicy, 33
      slaw, and tomato, 49
      sorbet, easy, 166
Maple syrup, in pork tenderloins in maple
      sauce, 128
Mayonnaise, prepared
      in artichoke dip, 30
      in easy cheesy potatoes, 59
Meatballs, prepared, in baked ravioli, 143
Meatloaf, Italian turkey, 76
Miracle Whip (ingredient), in pecan-crusted
      chicken with honey-mustard sauce, 134
Molly McButter (ingredient), in
      country garden Alfredo, 139
Mrs. Dash seasoning blend (ingredient), in
      country garden Alfredo, 139
Muffins
      blueberry pecan cluster, 22
      prepared, chocolate, in bread pudding
          with cherry sauce, 178
Mushrooms
      canned, in chicken cream topping, 133
      dried, in spinach bake, 64
      portabella, salad, and
          red chile vinaigrette, 62
      stuffed, crabmeat, 139
      stuffed, Italian, 25
Mustard, honey, in pecan-crusted chicken
      with honey-mustard sauce, 134

I N

Nacho ribs, 83
Nectarines
      French toast soufflé, 16
      in fresh fruit tart, 164
      in fruit tart, 164
      salad, with raspberry vinaigrette, 42

I O

Oatmeal, in harvest fruit bars, 23
Oatmeal raisin cookies, prepared,
      in pancakes, 17
Omelet, strawberry and ricotta cheese, 11
Onions
      red, in BBQ burgers in lettuce wraps, 150

Index I

sweet, in beef Napoleon, 150
Orange juice, in harvest fruit bars, 23

Oranges
    in ambrosia, Florida, 157
    breakfast knots, apple, 19
    in citrus salad with
    grilled shrimp adobo, 110
    clementines, delicious, 156
    salad, avocado and black olive, 43
    salad, spinach, 42

P

Paella, shrimp, 99
Pancakes, oatmeal raisin cookie, with maple
    syrup frosting, 17
Parfait, breakfast, 22
Pasta
    agnolotti, 80
    angel hair, with shrimp scampi, 110
    angel hair, with tomato chicken
    cream sauce, 143
    fettuccine, in crab scampi, 108
    fettuccine, salmon (canned), 90
    fettuccine, with salmon and dill
    Cheddar sauce, 115
    fettuccine, shrimp scampi, with asparagus
    and red bell pepper, 111
    noodles, in country garden Alfredo, 139
    penne all'arrabbiata, 99
    penne, in baked pasta with sausage
    and peppers, 77
    penne, herbed, and tuna, 96
    ravioli, prepared, baked
    (lasagna style), 143
    ravioli, prepared, fried, with
    pesto sauce, 145
    salad, avocado, bell pepper and
    feta cheese, 45
    in shrimp de Jonghe, 93
    spaghetti, in primavera pasta pie, 141
    spaghetti with tomatoes, toasted garlic
    and herbs, 97
Pasta sauce, prepared, in soup di Napoli, 56
Peaches
    crisp, 155
    in fresh fruit tart, 164

    in fruit tart, 164
    in galette, 168
Peanut butter, in chocolatey bars, 169
Pears
    Asian, with gingered pluot sauce, 157
    Asian, and pluot salad, 40
    balsamic chicken and, 134
    salad, southwest chicken and, 40
    sandwich, bacon cheese, 18
Peas
    in pilaf, 66
    sugar snap, oven roasted, 62
Pepperoni, in western bean salad, 48
Peppers, bell
    in baked pasta with sausage, 77
    in gazpacho, 53
    in relish, pickled, 66
    in sea scallops on summer succotash, 96
    stuffed, 67, 141
Peppers stuffed with tuna and
    salmon tartare, 28
Pesto, prepared, with fried ravioli, 145
Pico de gallo, 70
Pies
    apple, 162
    pumpkin, 163
Pilaf, peas, 66
Pineapple
    in fruit salad, tropical, 43
    in salad, festive party, 41
Pizza, prepared, mesquite-grilled chicken
    and artichoke, 138
Plums
    in fresh fruit tart, 164
    in fruit tart, 164
Pluots
    salad, Asian pear, 40
    sauce, gingered, with Asian pears, 157
Pocket Meals (ingredient), with salad, 148
Popcorn, oooey-gooey pull, 179
Pork
    baby back ribs, 129
    cassoulet, Mexican, with chipotle cream, 73
    loin, bacon-wrapped marinated, 81
    rack, mustard-pepper-crusted, 73
    ribs, nacho, 83
    tenderloin with cilantro lime pesto

    and smoky bacon bits, 83
    tenderloins in maple sauce, 128
Potatoes
    cakes, peanut, 60
    casserole, cheesy ranch, 61
    crab-stuffed twice-baked, 59
    easy cheesy, 59
    mashed, Cheddar, corn and salsa, 60
    salad, 50
    soup, slow-cooker, 54
    spinach and, au gratin, 61
Pound cake, prepared, in tiramisu, 172
Pugliese bread, prepared, in spicy crab melt, 26

Q

Quesadillas
    prepared, with spicy mango salsa, 33
    with roasted pepper &
    jalapeño hommus, 33
Quick bread mix, in caramel pumpkin cake, 174

R

Raisins, in rustic peach galette, 168
Ravioli, prepared
    baked (lasagna style), 143
    fried spinach cheese, with pesto sauce, 145
Relish
    pickled pepper, 66
    pico de gallo, 70
    roasted corn, 149
Rice
    pilaf, peas, 66
    pineapple sesame, 74
    risotto with asparagus and tomatoes, 103

S

Salad
    apple-crab, 38
    Asian pear and pluot, 40
    avocado fruit stand, 44
    bean, western, 48
    broccoli with maple-sesame dressing, 52
    cherry, with greens, 37
    cherry picnic, 37
    with chicken, garlic, 136
    chicken and pear, 40
    chicken salpicón, chipotle, 71

Chinese noodle and vegetable, 49

citrus, with grilled shrimp adobo, 110

creamy cranberry vinaigrette, 148

field greens, with turkey, 146

fruit, blueberry and mango, 103

fruit, festive party, 41

fruit, tropical, 43

grape tomato and avocado, 46

greens with cherry vinaigrette, 39

Jarlsberg sunset, 50

layered, with hearts of romaine, 47

mango and avocado, 46

mango citrus, with chile-crusted
sea scallops, 107

mushroom, portabella, and
red chile vinaigrette, 62

nectarine, with raspberry vinaigrette, 42

orange, avocado and black olive, 43

orange spinach, 42

pasta, avocado and bell pepper with
feta cheese, 45

potato, 50

red grape, grape tomato and
avocado, 105

shrimp, grilled, with citrus, 110

shrimp and vegetable, 93

slaw, tomato and mango, 49

spinach, cranberry almond, 38

spring mix with artichoke hearts and
roasted garlic, 47

spring mix, with feta, pecans and
strawberry vinaigrette, 48

vegetables, assorted (frozen), in
Normandy Blend salad, 51

Salad greens, prepackaged

Babé Farms Spring Mix, 48

Dole Romaine Salad Blend, 41

Earthbound Farm Spring Mix, 47

Ready Pac Grand Parisian Salad, 136

Salmon

baked in parchment, 116

chowder, and white fish, 91

fillets à la blanc, 113

grilled, with emerald kiwifruit salsa, 118

Modena, 112

Newburg, 114

orange/ginger, 117

and pasta with dill Cheddar sauce, 115

stuffed, with chipotle-lime aioli, 114

tartare, 90

Salmon, canned, fettuccine, 90

Salsa

corn and black bean, 32

kiwifruit, 118

mango, spicy, 33

prepared, in fiesta rice medley in sweet
bell peppers, 67

prepared, in western bean salad, 48

Sandwiches

chicken, pesto and pepper, 153

club, English muffin, 152

French dip, 101

ham and avocado, 153

pear and bacon cheese, 18

Sausage

hot link, in jambalaya, 148

Italian, in baked pasta, with peppers, 77

Italian, and bell pepper tacos, 142

Italian, and black bean soup, 57

Italian, kabobs, 76

Italian, in stuffed bell peppers, 141

Italian, turkey meatloaf, 76

kielbasa, in baked beans, 82

pork, in breakfast casserole, 15

pork, in sausage-cheese balls, 34

Scallops

with baby greens, 107

chile-crusted, with mango citrus
salad, 107

on summer succotash, 96

Scampi, prepared, in fettuccine with
asparagus and red bell pepper, 111

Shake 'n Bake (ingredient), in
pecan-crusted chicken, 134

Shrimp

bacon-wrapped, 25

chili lime, 27

coconut, prepared, with mustard
balsamic vinaigrette, 111

de Jonghe, 93

grilled adobo in citrus salad, 110

lime, prepared, in Caribbean dip, 29

paella, 99

salad, vegetable, 93

scampi with angel hair pasta, 110

scampi, prepared, in fettuccine with asparagus and red bell pepper, 111

Smoothies

berry, 183, 184

grape, 183

strawberry, 184

Snickers (ingredient), in cookie surprise, 180

Sole, lemon caper, 120

Soup, with chicken, pesto and
pepper sandwiches, 153

Soup mix

Bear Creek wild rice, in chicken roulade
with bacon, 136

Lipton onion, in artichoke dip, 30

Soups and stews

chowder, roasted corn and lobster, 94

chowder, salmon and white fish, 91

gazpacho, 53

gazpacho de almejas (clams), 53

gazpacho, fiery, 54

minestrone alla Fiorentina, 55

Napoli, 56

potato, slow-cooker, 54

sausage, Italian, and black bean, 57

spinach, celery, sausage and pasta, 56

veal stew, 131

Soymilk

in berry smoothie, 184

in strawberry smoothie, 184

Spinach

blue cheese flatbread, 34

frozen, in spinach bake, 64

and potatoes au gratin, 61

salad, cranberry almond, 38

salad, orange, 42

soup, celery, sausage and pasta, 56

Strawberries

crumble, double berry, 159

frozen, in smoothie, 184

tart, two-berry, with chocolate drizzle, 165

Sugar substitutes

Equal, in coffee latte, 186

Splenda No Calorie Sweetener, in
pumpkin pie, 163

Sweet'N Low, in mint crush, 185

Sushi, dipping sauces for, 28

Index **I**

I T

Tacos
    prepared, with spicy mango salsa, 33
    sausage and bell pepper, 142
    tilapia, 122

Taquitos, prepared, with bean sauce, 32

Tarts
    fresh fruit (peaches, nectarines,
    plums, grapes), 164
    fruit (plums, nectarines, peaches), 164
    two-berry, with chocolate drizzle, 165

Tea, iced apple, 185

Tilapia
    coconut fried fingers with mango
    ginger sauce, 123

Dijon, 122
    pesto, 123
    tacos, 122

Tomatoes
    in angel hair pasta with
    chicken cream sauce, 143
    canned, in corn and black bean salsa, 32
    crostini, 31
    in gazpacho, 53, 54
    grape, and avocado salad, 46
    grape, red grape and avocado salad, 105

    grape, in risotto with asparagus, 103
    in herbed penne and tuna, 96
    slaw, and mango, 49
    spaghetti with toasted garlic and herbs, 97

Tostada, breakfast, with Eggo waffles, 14

Trout, rainbow
    adobo with corn salsa, 124
    with shrimp cornbread stuffing, 124

Tuna, canned
    herbed penne and, 96
    kung pao, 151

Tuna, fresh
    hapa haole ahi, 118
    sesame-crusted grilled ahi, in ginger soy
    marinade, 119

Turkey
    breast, prepared, in festive
    field greens, 146

I V

Veal
    chops, grilled, with sage jus, 129
    chops with mustard sage sauce, 130
    cutlets Cordon Bleu, 131
    stew, 131

Vegetables
    assorted (frozen), in

    Normandy Blend salad, 51
    stir-fry (frozen), in rotisserie
    chicken stir-fry, 137

Velveeta (ingredient),
    in easy cheesy potatoes, 59

Vinaigrette
    cherry, 39
    cranberry, creamy, 148
    raspberry, 42
    red chile, 62

I W

Waffles, frozen, in breakfast tostada, 14

Watermelon, in fruit bowl with
    raspberry vinaigrette, 20

Wild Blueberry Pecan Cluster Cereal (ingredient)
    in breakfast parfait, 22
    in muffins, 22

Wraps, Hawaiian, with spiral-cut ham, 82

I Y

Yogurt
    in berry smoothie, 183, 184
    in breakfast parfait, 22
    dessert bars, cherry-almond, 176
    in strawberry smoothie, 184

ACONEX, *156*
www.aconex.cl
011-56-2-9413312

ALL STATE PACKERS, *40*
www.rivermaid.com
209-369-3586

ALPINE FRESH, *102, 103*
www.alpinefresh.com

ALSUM PRODUCE, *54*
www.alsum.com
larry.alsum@alsum.com
800-236-5127

AMERICA'S KITCHEN, *139*
www.americaskitchen.com
info@americaskitchen.com
770-754-0707

AMERICAN PRIDE
SEAFOODS, *p. 107*
www.americanprideseafoods.com
800-343-8046

ANNE'S HOUSE OF NUTS, *63*
301-317-0900

ANTHONY FARMS, *54*
www.anthonyfarms.com
800-826-0456

APIO/EAT SMART, *52*
www.apioinc.com
800-626-2746

APPLE & EVE, *186*
www.appleandeve.com
info@appleandeve.com
800-969-8018

AQUACHILE, *112*
www.aquachile.com
rsquadritto@aquachile.com
954-659-0955

AQUAFARMS, *116*
www.aquafarms.com
info@aquafarms.com
305-364-0009

AQUAGOLD SEAFOOD, *118*
www.aquastar.com
206-448-5400

AQUASTAR, *108*

ARTHUR SCHUMAN, *141*
www.arthurschuman.com
973-227-0030

ASSOCIATED FRUIT, *40*
scott@piggypears.com
541-535-1787

ATLANTIC CAPES
FISHERIES, *106, 107*
508-990-9040

ATLANTIC VEAL & LAMB, *130, 131*
718-599-6400

AUSTRALIAN LAMB, *86, 87, 88*
www.auslamb.com
shane@auslamb.com

BABÉ FARMS, *48*
www.babefarms.com
customerservice@babefarms.com
800-648-6772

BARRY CALLEBAUT, *173*
www.barry-callebaut.com
stalbans@barry-callebaut.com
802-524-9711

BASIN GOLD, *60*
www.basingold.com
sales@basingold.com
509-545-4161

BC HOTHOUSE, *95, 96, 97*
www.bchothouse.com
800-663-1889

BEAR CREEK, *136*
www.bearcreekfoods.com
cservice@bearcreekfoods.com
435-654-6415

BEE SWEET CITRUS, *42*
www.beesweetcitrus.com
559-834-5345

BELGIOIOSO CHEESE, *144*
www.belgioioso.com
920-863-2123

BEST BRANDS/
MULTIFOODS, *172, 178*
www.multifoods.com
www.bestbrandscorp.com
800-866-3300
800-328-2068

BOLTHOUSE FARMS, *171*
www.bolthouse.com
661-366-7201

BONITA BANANA, *173*
800-588-2228

BOSKOVICH FARMS, *38*
www.boskovichfarms.com
marketing@boskovichfarms.com
805-487-2299

BOUNTY FRESH, *43*
www.bountyfresh.com
sales@bountyfresh.com
305-592-6969

BRAWLEY BEEF, *126*
www.brawleybeef.com

CALAVO GROWERS, *44, 45*
www.calavo.com
800-4-CALAVO (22-5286)

CAMANCHACA, *117*
www.camanchacainc.com
800-335-7553

CAMPBELL'S, *153*
www.campbellselect.com
800-257-8443

CARDILE BROTHERS, *24, 25*
cardilebro@aol.com
610-268-2470

CARGILL MEAT
SOLUTIONS, *100, 101*
www.cargillmeatsolutions.com
877-596-4069

CATTLEMEN'S, *129*
www.frenchsfoodservice.com
800-442-4733

CHELAN FRESH, *160*
www.chelanfresh.com
509-682-3854

CHICKEN OF THE SEA, *151*
www.chickenofthesea.com

CIBO NATURALS, *145*
www.cibonaturals.com
800-823-2426

CLEAR SPRINGS, *124*
www.clearsprings.com
csf@clearsprings.com
800-635-8211

COLUMBIA MARKETING
INTERNATIONAL, *162*
www.cmiapples.com
509-663-1955

CONAGRA, *27,58,59,149,179*
www.conagrafoods.com
www.conagraseafood.com
813-241-1500

COUNTRYSIDE BAKING, *168*
800-478-4252

DAMASCUS, *50*
www.damascusbakery.com
sales@damascusbakery.com
800-367-7482

DANNON, *183*
www.dannon.com
877-326-6668

DARE FOODS, *31*
www.darefoods.com
800-668-3273

D'ARRIGO BROS. OF CA, *47*
www.andyboy.com
800-995-5939

DEL MONTE, *32*
www.delmonte.com

DEL MONTE FRESH
PRODUCE COMPANY, *163*
Jbohmer@freshdelmonte.com
305-520-8118

DELANO FARMS, *104, 105*
delfarm@delanofarmsco.com
661-721-1485

DEL REY AVOCADO, *44, 45*
760-728-8325

Vendor listing **I**

DELTA PRIDE, *125*
www.deltapride.com

DENICE & FILICE, LLC, *150*
www.denicefilice.com
831-630-6000

DIAMOND FRUIT GROWERS, *18*
www.diamondfruit.com
541-354-5300

DNE FRUIT, *157*
www.dneworld.com
800-327-6676

DOLE, *41*
www.dole.com
800-232-8888

DOMEX, *158*
www.superapple.com
info@superapple.com
509-966-1866

DON MIGUEL
MEXICAN FOODS, *33*
www.donmiguel.com
714-634-8441

EARTHBOUND FARM, *47*
www.ebfarm.com
info@ebfarm.com
800-690-3200

EGGLAND'S BEST, *11*
www.eggland.com

EL MONTEREY, *146*
www.elmonterey.com
contactus@ruizfoods.com
800-477-6474

EQUAL SWEETENER/
MERISANT CORP., *186*
www.merisant.com
312-840-6000

EUROFRESH FARMS, *49*
www.eurofresh.com
comments@eurofresh.com
520-384-4621

EVERGOOD FINE FOODS, *148*
www.evergoodfoods.com
415-822-4660

FISH HOUSE FOODS, *114*
760-597-1270

FISHER CAPESPAN, *43*
www.fishercapespan.com
info@shercapespan.com
800-388-3074

FJORD SEAFOOD USA, *113*
www.fjordseafoodamericas.com
800-780-FISH (3474)

FOSTER FARMS, *69, 70, 71*
www.fosterfarms.com
800-255-7227

FOUR STAR FRUIT, *182, 183*
661-725-0186

FOWLER PACKING, *164*
www.fowlerpacking.com
559-834-5911

FOXY FOODS, *49*
www.foxy.com
800-695-5012

FRESKA PRODUCE, *46*
www.freskaproduce.com
sales@freskaproduce.com
805-650-1040

GENERAL MILLS/BISQUICK, *34*
www.bisquick.com
bettycrocker.response@
genmills.com
800-446-1898

GENERAL MILLS/YOPLAIT, *176*
www.yoplaitusa.com
800-967-5248

GEORGE WESTON BAKERIES, *152*
www.gwbakeries.com
800-356-3314

GIORGIO FOODS, *133*
www.giorgiofoods.com
customerservice@
giorgiofoods.com
610-926-2139

GIUMARRA, *44, 45*
www.giumarra.com
760-480-8502

GLOBAL BERRY FARMS, *159, 165*
www.globalberryfarms.com
239-591-1664

GOLD KIST FARMS, *78, 79 80*
www.goldkist.com
866-GK FARMS (453-2767)

GRACE BAKING, *26*
800-550-6810

GRIMMWAY FARMS, *171*
www.grimmway.com
661-845-9435

GROWER DIRECT, *154, 155, 170*
www.growerdirect.net
209-931-7900

HANNAH INTERNATIONAL, *33*
www.hannahfoods.net
603-474-5805

HASS AVOCADO BOARD, *44, 45*
www.avocadocentral.com
949-341-3250

HEINZ, *32, 35, 56, 135*
www.heinz.com
800-255-5750

HELLMANN'S/BEST FOODS, *30*
www.homebasics.com
201-894-4000

HOLTZINGER FRUIT, *176*
www.holtzingerfruit.com
509-457-5115

HORMEL, *48*
www.hormel.com

IDAHO TROUT, *124*
www.idahotrout.com
rainbowtrout@idahotrout.com
866-878-7688

INDEX FRESH, *44, 45*
www.indexfresh.com
admin@indexfresh.com
909-877-0999

J&J SNACK FOODS, *17*
www.jjsnack.com

JELLY BELLY, *181*
www.jellybelly.com
mrjellybelly@jellybelly.com
800-522-3267

JENNIE-O TURKEY STORE, *146*
www.j-ots.com
800-621-3505

JON DONAIRE DESSERTS, *174*
www.jondonaire.com
877-DONAIRE (366-2473)

KELLOGG'S, *14*
www.kelloggs.com
consumer-affairs@kellogg.com
800-962-0052

KEYSTONE, *150*
www.keystonefruit.com
717-597-2112

KINGSBURG ORCHARDS, *40, 157*
www.kingsburgorchards.com
sales@kingsburgorchards.com
559-897-2986

KIRKLAND SIGNATURE GARLIC
BUTTER FLATBREAD, *34*
www.c2b.com
800-266-2782

KIRKLAND SIGNATURE MEAT
LASAGNA, *55*

KIRKLAND SIGNATURE TAKE
AND BAKE PIZZA, *138*

KIRKLAND SIGNATURE STIR FRY
VEGETABLES, *137*
800-491-2665

KIRKLAND SIGNATURE/
CLIFFSTAR CORPORATION, *184*
www.cliffstar.com
800-777-2389

KIRKLAND SIGNATURE/
NEWMAN'S OWN, *22*
www.newmansown.com

KIRKLAND SIGNATURE/
NUTRIVERDE, 51
800-491-2665

KIRKLAND SIGNATURE/
PURATOS, 175
www.puratos.us
infous@puratos.com
856-428-4300

KIRKLAND SIGNATURE/
SARA LEE COFFEE & TEA, 21
www.saraleecoffeetea.com
800-373-6705

KIRKLAND SIGNATURE/
SEVIROLI FOODS, 143
www.sevirolifoods.com
516-222-6220

KIRKLAND SIGNATURE/SILK, 184
www.silkissoy.com

KIRSCHENMAN, 20
559-741-7030

KRAFT, 59, 134
www.kraftfoods.com

KRUSTEAZ, 174
www.krusteaz.com

L & M, 147, 161
www.lmcompanies.com

LA BREA BAKERY, 153
www.labreabakery.com
info@labreabakery.com
818-742-4242

LEGEND PRODUCE, 43
www.legendproduce.com
623-298-3782

LIPTON, 30
www.homebasics.com
201-894-4000

LOS ANGELES SALAD
COMPANY, 65
www.lasalad.com
customerservice@lasalad.com
626-322-9000

LT OVERSEAS LTD, INC., 66
www.daawatbasmati.com
732-661-1030

M & R, 21
mrpack@inreach.com
209-369-2725

MACK FARMS, 61
mcmelon@aol.com
863-692-1200

MANN'S, 62
www.mannpacking.com
800-884-MANN (6226)

MAPLE LEAF, 25
www.mapleleaf.ca
johnsoda@mapleleaf.ca
916-863-3468

MARGARITAVILLE
SHRIMP, 29, 111
www.margaritavilleshrimp.com
info@margaritavilleshrimp.com
800-339-1533

MARIANI, 30
www.mariani.com
800-672-8655

MARINE HARVEST, 89, 90, 91
www.marineharvest.com

MAS MELONS & GRAPES, 20
520-377-2372

MAZZETTA COMPANY,
LLC., 92, 93, 94
www.mazzetta.com
seamazz@mazzetta.com
847-433-1150

McCORMICK, 98, 99
www.mccormick.com
800-322-SPICE

McDANIEL AVOCADO, 44, 45
www.mcdanielavocado.com
760-728-8438

METZ FRESH, 56
www.metzfresh.com
831-759-4805

MICHAEL FOODS, 11,12
www.michaelfoods.com
952-258-4000

MILTON'S, 16
www.miltonsbaking.com
858-350-9696

MISSION PRODUCE, 44, 45
www.missionpro.com
800-549-3420

MONSTER BEVERAGE CO., 149
866-322-4466

MONTEREY GOURMET
FOODS, 145
www.montereygourmet
foods.com
800-588-7782

MONTEREY MUSHROOMS, 62
www.montereymushrooms.com
831-763-5300

MOUNTAIN STREAM
TILAPIA, 122
www.mountainstreamtilapia.com
866-691-7997

MOUNTAIN VIEW FRUIT
SALES, 164
www.summeripe.com
info@summeripe.com
559-351-5321

MOZZARELLA FRESCA, 35
www.mozzarellafresca.com
sales@mozzarellafresca.com
800-572-6818

MRS. DASH &
MOLLY MCBUTTER, 139
www.mrsdash.com
www.mollymcbutter.com
800-622-3274

NATURE SWEET, 46
www.naturesweettomatoes.com
800-315-8209

NEW YORK APPLE, 161
ed@newyorkapplesales.com
518-477-7200

NEW WORLD RESTAURANT
GROUP, 13
www.nwrgi.com

NEW YORK STYLE
SAUSAGE, 140, 141
www.newyorkstylesausage.com
408-745-7675

NEW STAR, 61
www.newstarfresh.com
info@newstarfresh.com
831-758-7800

NORCO RANCH, 12, 13
www.norcoeggs.com
800-373-1692

NORSELAND, 50
www.norseland.com
800-326-5620

NORTH COAST SEAFOODS, 120
617-345-4400

NUCAL FOODS, 12, 13
www.nucalfoods.com
209-254-2200

OCEAN MIST FARMS, 64
www.oceanmist.com
831-633-2144

OKAMI, 28
www.okamifoods.com
service@okamifoods.com
888-922-6833

OLD FASHIONED MAPLE
CREST, 128
www.bernards.ca
nancy@bernards.ca
418-588-6109

OPPENHEIMER, 54
www.oppyproduce.com

OREGON CHAI, 180
www.oregonchai.com

ORIGINAL NUT HOUSE, 63
www.originalnuthouse.com
800-726-7222

Vendor listing I

P&L IMPORTS /
GAROFALO, 98, 99
www.pandlimports.com
866-327-2782

PACIFIC SEAFOOD, 26, 109
www.pacseafood.com

PERDUE FARMS
INCORPORATED, 84, 85
www.perdue.com
800-4-PERDUE (473-7383)

PENNSYLVANIA APPLE
BOARD, 161
www.pennsyapples.org
support@pennsyapples.org
717-783-5418

PHILLIPS, 108
www.phillipsfoods.com
comments@phillipsfoods.com
888-234-CRAB (2722)

POCKET MEALS, 148
www.chefamerica.com
800-350-5016

PPCS LIMITED, 151
www.ppcs.co.nz
sales@ppcs.co.nz
64-3-477-3980

PREMIO, 57, 142
www.premiofoods.com
info@premiofoods.com
973-427-1106

PRIMAVERA, 39
www.primafrutta.com
primav2@att.global.net
209-931-9420

PRIME TIME INTERNATIONAL, 66
www.primetimeproduce.com
760-399-4166

PROFOOD USA, 138
www.profoodcorp.com
sales@profoodcorp.com

QUAKER, 23
www.quakeroatmeal.com
800-856-5781

RAIN FOREST
AQUACULTURE, 123
www.tilapia.com
sales@tilapia.com
800-289-8452

RAINIER FRUIT COMPANY, 37
www.rainierfruit.com

READY PAC, 136, 166, 177
www.readypac.com
800-800-4088

REGAL SPRINGS, 123
www.regalsprings.com
941-747-9161

REYNOLDS, 127
www.reynoldskitchens.com
800-433-2244

RICHARD BAGDASARIAN, 167
www.mrgrape.com
760-396-2168

RIO MAR, 122
www.enaca.net
sales@enacausa.com
800-569-8323

RUSSET POTATO EXCHANGE, 54
www.rpespud.com
800-678-2789

SAGE FRUIT, 159
www.sagefruit.com
509-248-5828

SAN FRANCISCO BAY, 187
www.sfbcoffee.com
800-829-1300

SARA LEE FOODS, 15
www.saralee.com

SCHREIBER FOODS, 29
www.schreiberfoods.com
800-344-0333

SEALD SWEET, 110
www.sealdsweet.com
info@sealdsweet.com
800-237-7525

SEAPAK, 111
800-654-9731

SEA WATCH, 53
www.seawatch.com
sales@seawatch.com
410-822-7500

SHIITAKE-YA, 64
www.shiitakeya.com

SKAGIT VALLEY'S
BEST PRODUCE, 60
www.svbest.com
sales@svbest.com
360-848-0777

SMITHFIELD, 81, 82, 83
www.smithfieldfoods.com
888-366-6767

SMITHFIELD BEEF, 128

SMOKI FOODS, 114
206-243-9650

SMUCKER'S, 169
www.crisco.com
www.jif.com

SNICKERS, 180
www.marsbrightideas.com

SOUSA SEAFOOD, 120
www.sousaseafood.com
sousaseafood@aol.com
617-428-6976

SOUTH FLORIDA POTATO
GROWERS EXCHANGE, 61
Flspuds@cfl.rr.com
800-830-7783

SPLENDA, 163
www.splenda.com
800-7-SPLENDA (7753632)

STARBUCKS, 188
www.starbucks.com

STEMILT GROWERS, 36, 37
www.stemilt.com
509-662-9667

STEVCO, 167
www.grapeman.com
661-392-1719

SUGAR BOWL BAKERY, 178
www.sugarbowlbakery.com
415-824-3592

SUGAR FOODS, 185
www.sugarfoods.com
912-966-1005

SUNKIST, 132, 133
www.sunkist.com
aschierling@sunkistgrowers.com
818-986-4800

SUNNY COVE, 19
www.sccitrus.com
559-626-4085

SUN-MAID RAISIN, 168
www.sunmaid.com

SUNDATE, 166
Sundate@hotmail.com
760-398-6123

SUNSET/MASTRONARDI
PRODUCE, 67, 143
www.sunsetproduce.com
info@sunsetproduce.com
519-326-3218

SUNWEST, 155
www.sunwestfruit.com
sales@sunwestfruit.com
559-646-4400

SWIFT & COMPANY, 72, 73, 74
www.swiftbrands.com
emailus@swiftbrands.com
800-727-2333

TANIMURA & ANTLE, INC., 150
www.taproduce.com
800-772-4542

TARANTINO, 75, 76, 77
619-232-7585

TILLAMOOK COUNTRY
CREAMERY ASSOC., 115
www.tillamookcheese.com
503-842-4481

TJ KRAFT, 118
www.norpacexport.com
tjkraft@norpacexport.com
808-842-3474

TOP BRASS, 50
www.topbrassmarketing.com
661-746-2148

TREE TOP, 185
www.treetop.com
800-542-4055

TRIDENT SEAFOODS, 121
www.tridentseafoods.com
800-SEALEGS (732-5347)

TRINITY FRUIT, 42
www.trinityfruit.com
sales@trinityfruit.com
559-433-3777

TROPICANA, 23
www.tropicana.com
800-237-7799

TYSON, 127, 134, 135
www.tyson.com
800-233-6332

VALLEY PRIDE, 60
Sales@valleypridesales.com
360-428-2717

VENTURA FOODS, LLC, 110
www.venturafoods.com

VIE DE FRANCE, 18
www.vdfy.com
800-446-4404

WALLACE FARMS, 60
sales@wallacespuds.com
360-757-0981

WESPAK, 16
www.wespak.com
sales@wpemail.com
559-897-4800

WEST PAK, 44, 45
www.westpakavocado.com
matt@westpakavocado.com
951-296-5757

*WESTERN SWEET
CHERRY, 154,155*
509-972-4476

*WESTERN UNITED FISH
COMPANY, 119*
www.wufco.net
westernunited@wufco.net
206-763-1227

WILCOX FARMS, 12, 13
www.wilcoxfarms.com

WILSONBATIZ, 28, 53
www.wilsonbatiz.com
619-661-5222

WINDSET FARMS, 54
www.windsetfarms.com

*WOLVERINE PACKING
COMPANY, 129*
www.wolverinepacking.com
800-521-1390

YAKIMA-ROCHE FRUIT, 38
509-453-4000

Notes